How to Climb 5.12

Praise for the first edition:

"*How to Climb 5.12* packs a lot into a slim book . . . a great first training book and a good addition to any training junkie's book shelf."

— *Rock & Ice* magazine

"Eric Hörst is a writer whose books are concise, informative and easily digestible. *How to Climb 5.12* isn't just for those who are experienced in the sport, but also offers a great deal to those just starting out as the prin ciples are very scalable."

— Deadpoint Climbing Online, United Kingdom

A FALCON GUIDE®

HOW TO CLIMB SERIES

How to Climb 5.12

SECOND EDITION

Eric J. Hörst

FALCON®

GUILFORD, CONNECTICUT
HELENA, MONTANA

AN IMPRINT OF THE GLOBE PEQUOT PRESS

To my brother, Kyle,
for introducing me to this outrageous sport!

AFALCONGUIDE®

Page design: Casey Shain
Photos by the author unless otherwise indicated
ISSN 1546-0746
ISBN 0-7627-2576-1

Manufactured in the United States of America
Second Edition/Second Printing

Contents

Acknowledgments

I would like to thank everyone who in some way contributed to or helped produce *How to Climb 5.12*. Excellent photography and artwork grace the pages throughout—thanks to Chris Falkenstein, Stewart Green, Mike Landkroon, Eric McCallister, Mike McGill, Michael Miller, and Sean Michael. A few gyms and climbers enthusiastically helped in producing the instructional photos—thanks to Climbnasium, Philadelphia Rock Gym, and Vertical Extreme, and to Bob Africa, John Boschetti, L. A. Hörst, Matt Kellerman, Scott Mechler, Tom Muller, Brinda Salla, and Bruce Stick. Also, many thanks to Russ Clune, Mark Robinson, Steve Petro, Jay McElwain, Andrzej Malewicz, and Bob Perna for the early read-throughs and invaluable feedback. And to the companies that support me and my efforts—Nicros, La Sportiva, and Sterling Ropes—you are all great.

Finally, to my wife, Lisa Ann, and to my parents—thanks for unconditional love, support, and late-night proofreading. Thanks to my training partners, the hometown boys, LIVE, and Out Of The Gray for the best training tunes around! And to Gayle and Dave Plecha for the postwriting refuge in RPV.

Jany Mitges on AWOL (5.10c), Roadside
Crag, Red River Gorge, Kentucky.
PHOTO: MIKE LANDKROON

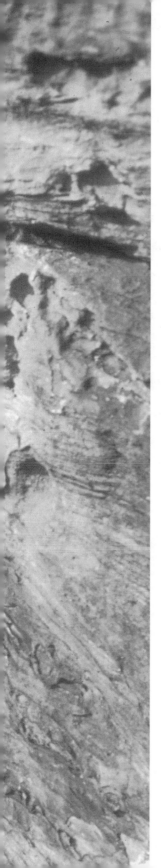

Introduction

Life is short. You should aim at what you feel most like doing. —Patrick Edlinger

A better title for this book might be *How to Become a Better Climber—Fast!* After all, performing better is the goal of participants in most sports, whether a golfer wanting to lower his handicap or a runner training to run her personal-best race. In the sport of climbing, 5.12 has become known as the sort of door to elite levels. For years 5.12 ascents were a rare feat achieved by few. Although more common today, 5.12 is still a magical grade, and chances are you have what it takes to get there. But how can you get there most quickly?

Given the recent glut of climbing books on the market, it's hard to find time to digest and utilize all the material. Although I'm adding to that glut with this book, *How to Climb 5.12* offers a fresh, streamlined approach to elevating your performance on the rock—fast!

The following pages serve up a wide range of powerful *and*

practical strategies for pushing your limits in the days and seasons to come. You will learn climbing-specific strength- and fitness-training exercises, effective drills for honing climbing skills, powerful mental-training techniques, and numerous redpoint strategies as used by the world's best climbers. While you may recognize some familiar ideas, I expect you'll discover a wealth of new ones that will energize and empower you to climb better, beginning today!

This book is based on my better than two decades as a climber and performance coach. Over the years I've reviewed countless peer-review publications on motor learning and sport performance, studied and developed leading-edge mental-training strategies, and spent countless days experimenting with and refining new training methods (when I should have been out climbing). In aggregate this text is the most condensed, practical instruction for improving your climbing available.

Although *How To Climb 5.12* presents dozens of powerful skill-, fitness-, and mental-training strategies, it does not offer in-depth instruction on specific moves or safety techniques. Read John Long's *How to Rock Climb* and *Climbing Anchors* for excellent and entertaining technical instruction. Consult *Training for Climbing* for a comprehensive and scientific look at all the issues that affect climbing performance.

Finally, I want to comment that I was a bit hesitant to use the 5.12 grade in the title of this book. I'm a firm believer that the difficulty of a climb is secondary to the simple pleasure of pulling down on some good stone. Still, it would be a lie to say that the lust to climb ever-more-difficult routes is not a strong motivator for most. Breaking barriers, achieving dreams, and the intense rush of doing an outrageous route is part of the spirit of this sport. And it is killer fun!

With this in mind, I want to add that your trip to 5.12 (and beyond) must always be fun. If it ever starts to feel like a job, then it's time to take a few weeks off. Savor the successes, failures, and all the hard work during your journey, and vow to enjoy every climb regardless of the grade. Drop me a note when you send your first 5.12 or experience some other major breakthrough. Be safe and God bless.

Ian Spencer-Green on
Bullet the Blue Sky
(5.12d), Penitente
Canyon, Colorado.
PHOTO: STEWART GREEN

CHAPTER ONE

Yes, You Can Climb 5.12!

Climbing is an incredibly complex sport. It's not just a matter of strength. There are mental factors to consider as well as motivation, technique, experience and confidence. —Tony Yaniro

I f you are reading this book, chances are you have what it takes to climb 5.12. Regardless of age or current ability, most climbers I meet do indeed have the potential to succeed at this difficult grade. I've met people of all shapes and sizes, ages and professions who regularly climb 5.12. In fact, the 5.12 climbers I know range from preteen girls to retired grandparents. Undoubtedly you can, too—if you make a resolute decision to climb 5.12, develop and follow an intelligent plan, and remain focused and disciplined despite occasional frustration or apparent roadblocks.

The two things stopping most people from reaching the grade are lack of accurate information on how to get there and periodic lapses in motivation or discipline. Although the latter items have to come from inside you, the how-to-get-there information is available in heavy doses right here, right now.

Getting On Route to 5.12

Most people unknowingly get lost long before reaching 5.12 due to a combination of trial-and-error learning and misinformation. Ultimately, this approach will have you climbing to a dead end.

As a metaphor, suppose you wanted to climb the Nose of El Capitan in Yosemite but had no guidebook, beta, line of fixed gear, or chalked holds to follow. All you knew was that the climb went somewhere up the literal nose of El Cap. How successful would you be? Initially, you'd probably succeed at getting a pitch or two off the ground somewhere on the Nose. Your confidence would skyrocket as you figured to be on route! Right? But looming above are many cracks and corners. Which to take now? Do you need to pendulum to another line? Unfortunately, without an accurate guide you'd never know the correct route up. Progress slows, and eventually you hit a dead end.

This scenario parallels the story line of many a climber's journey toward 5.12. Huge amounts of invested energy and time result in ever-decreasing gains in ability. Eventually, progress becomes negligible as climbing ability plateaus short of 5.12.

Distinguishing Good Advice from Bad Advice

In an effort to break through the plateau, it's natural to want to seek and load up on any information and advice you can wring out of other climbers. Some common advice you are likely to hear: "Wear tighter shoes, climb a lot, do lots of pull-ups, join a gym, work on projects, get even tighter shoes, do more pull-ups, eat fewer calories and lose weight, do more pull-ups, hang on a finger-board, train harder, climb some more, start campus training, eat even less, climb even more . . ."

Unfortunately, this mindless, shoot-from-the-hip approach will yield about the same results as trying to climb El Cap without a guidebook. It lacks an intelligent plan based on facts, and it suffers from the childish mentality that "if some is good, more must be better." If climbing three days a week is good, then climbing six days a week is twice as good. If dieting is good, then a crash diet is better. Obviously, these theories are flawed, but there are a surprising number of climbers enamored of them.

The good news is that there are certain facts and theories that apply equally to all human beings. In medicine a vaccine that works on one human being will work on all human beings. Or with respect to diet, if I eat more calories than I burn, I will get fat, and if you eat more calories than you burn, you will get fat. Likewise, there are training absolutes and motor learning theories (about how we acquire complex skills) that are valid for all human beings. If we understand these principles and follow them, then we will get similar results.

Certainly, we all have unique DNA that defines each of us. We all have slightly different genetic potential, which means different starting and ending points in terms of absolute climbing ability. But I believe the end point of the envelope of potential is beyond 5.12a for most individuals.

Nine Absolute Truths of Climbing Performance

Detailed below are nine absolutes of climbing performance that provide a foundation for this text. In the following chapters you'll see these absolutes give birth to many subprinciples and practice techniques that are supremely effective. Develop your training program accordingly, and the trip to 5.12 will be faster than you think!

Absolute 1:

The best training for climbing skill (technique and tactics) is climbing.

This first absolute might seem obvious, but it surprises me how many people act in a manner contrary to this principle. The concept of cross-training does not apply to sport skills as complex as climbing. Time spent doing any other sport

Bouldering is a highly effective method of learning skills and developing focus and strength. Climber sending King Tut (V5) at Governor Stable, Pennsylvania.

with the thought that it "might help my climbing" is time wasted. There are simply no other sports with technical and tactical requirements anywhere similar to climbing.

Although there may be some minor transfer of the fitness conditioning gained by doing other sports, there will be no gain in skill. Even activities that seem to have something in common with climbing (like the balance required for gymnastics or walking a slack line) transfer no skill to the vertical plane.

Sure, variety is the spice of life. If your goal is to become an ace on the rock, however, it's your time spent climbing that will get you there. Invest what playtime you have on this sport and dabble in all the rest only on your days off or during rest periods between training cycles.

Absolute 2:
Climbing skills are specific to rock type, angle, and frictional properties.

Climbing may be a natural activity, but the skills required for proficiency in this sport are as complex as any other. There are literally thousands of different climbing areas with likely millions of different routes. Each route possesses slightly different character and form, requiring you to execute somewhat different techniques and tactics in every case.

Climbing movements may be similar from one climb to the next, but the actual moves feel different due to variations in rock type, angle, and frictional properties. Skill is therefore very sensitive and specific to the infinite variations in our "playing field." You have lived the proof of this principle, I'm sure.

We're all familiar with the phenomenon of the indoor "prince of plastic" who instantly transforms into a pauper on real rock (the opposite is also common). People who excel on slab climbs are often mediocre on vertical or overhanging rock. You may even know a local "rock star" who can shred 5.11s on his turf but gets spanked on 5.10s while on a road trip. The classic example is the crack master who flails on face climbs, and the sport climber who couldn't jam a handcrack for a million bucks.

Of course, the best climbers perform well in almost any situation and at most areas. They climb at an exceedingly high level because they have programmed gazillions of different moves that are on call at a moment's notice. Consequently, they can react quickly, and often intuitively, to even the most novel moves and sequences. This is your goal, and climbing at many different areas is the means. Start driving.

Absolute 3:
Skill practice yields a greater return on investment than fitness training for all but elite climbers.

The learning curve for climbing skill is steeper and continues upward longer and more steadily than a curve showing gains in climbing strength from fitness training. Period. If you have a limited amount of time to invest in training and climbing, it would be wise to use that time actually climbing instead of fitness training.

In business it's called return on investment. It goes like this: You have $100 to invest on two possible investments. One guarantees a payback of $200 in just one month, the other may pay back $125 . . . if you're lucky. Where do you put your money? Should you split it between the two? Of course not. Put it all in the first investment!

In climbing, training skill is the surefire investment. Like the first investment in the previous example, steady gains are guaranteed. Time put into strength training (like investment two above) may yield gradual gains but with nowhere near the rate and certainty of training skill.

Elite climbers with highly honed skills are the exception. Their investment "money" is better placed on strength training (due to some strange market force!).

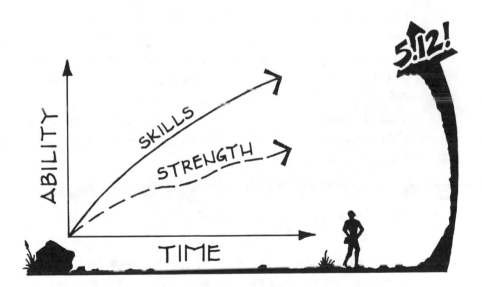

For most people, time spent climbing is far more important—and provides faster gains in ability—than strength training.

Absolute 4:

General conditioning is the most effective type of fitness training for beginner-level climbers.

Okay, so you're a beginner-level climber with the time and desire to do some strength training. Invest your time in becoming an all-around well-conditioned physical specimen such as Steph Davis or Tommy Caldwell, not an Arnold look-alike (Tom *or* Schwarzenegger!). Your goal is to minimize body fat and unnecessary muscle mass, because both will pull you down. You also want to tune up all your muscles, particularly those used in pulling motions. Perform a moderate amount of aerobic training—running is ideal—to drop the fat and reduce bulky muscles. Or if you're skinny and feel that you lack overall muscular tone, it would be wise to begin some moderate-intensity circuit or free-weight training two or three days per week.

For now, don't worry about developing fingers of steel. Sport-specific exercises such as fingerboard training, campus training, and hypergravity training are inappropriate at this time and may result in injury.

Absolute 5:

Sport-specific conditioning is the most effective fitness training for advanced climbers.

The most difficult routes often require heroic feats of strength in situations where even perfect technique isn't enough to win. If you're very solid on 5.10 and possess all-around conditioning and technique, then some sport-specific strength training should be added to your program. Increased pulling power and developing a viselike grip are your goals.

Cut back or eliminate general conditioning and execute an intelligent strength-training program that addresses your limiting weaknesses. Progress deep into the 5.12 grade depends on it.

Absolute 6:

Strength training builds endurance, but endurance training does not build maximum strength.

Your sport-specific fitness training must focus first and foremost on building maximum strength, particularly in the arms and forearms. Obviously, with this higher level of strength you will be better prepared for the most savage crux sequences. But that's not all. On the many submaximal moves throughout the rest of a climb, you'll be able to use a lower percentage of maximum strength. This means more endurance!

Unfortunately, endurance training will not benefit your maximum strength even 1 percent. It comes down to return on your training investment. In this case the big money lies in training maximum strength.

Absolute 7:
Wasted energy and time are lost forever.

The quickest way to increase apparent strength and endurance is not through training but by reducing wasted energy while climbing. Of course, it's impossible to quantify the amount of energy the average climber needlessly expends on a route; I would guess it's in the ballpark of 50 percent. If I'm anywhere close on this estimate, there's a huge windfall of strength awaiting the climber who makes a conscious effort to end this "overcharge."

Your climbing skill (technique and tactics), or lack thereof, is at the heart of this matter. Climb too slow, grip too hard, use poor body positioning, miss a hold, and you'll use far more energy than required. This highlights the value of Absolute 3, which states the high importance of training skill.

Your mind is also a powerful tool in the quest to conserve energy. Acute awareness of energy leaks and poise in the midst of battle are two characteristics of champion climbers. Reaching 5.12 will be difficult and painful without them.

Absolute 8:
Your body cannot go where the mind has not gone first.

Almost every elite athlete, in every sport, in every country uses visualization as a performance-enhancing tool. Period. Whether it's Lance Armstrong visualizing the strategy for winning another Tour de France or Chris Sharma visualizing his next 5.14 send, big successes at big things cannot come without it.

Visualization prepares a mental blueprint for action and thus the framework for reality. It must be as factual, detailed, and positive as possible if it is to give birth to the desired results. Certainly many failures have been preprogrammed by poor-quality visualization based on erroneous information, negative thoughts, and unreasonable fears. Only through daily use in a wide range of applications will you master this skill.

Begin using visualization before important tasks, whether a speech at school, a project at work, or a fix-up at home. Create a full-color mental movie of the best course of action, and always end it with a vivid image of the ideal outcome.

Absolute 9:

Training and climbing provide stimulus for, but no actual, muscular growth. Recomposition and strengthening occur only during sleep and on rest days.

Your muscles become stronger and your nervous system adapts to new moves and demands during rest periods, not during exercise. Although climbing and training are the stimulus for growth, they are actually catabolic, meaning they break down your body. The quality and quantity of your recovery time is thus just as important as your training and climbing time.

Supercompensation requires specific macronutrients as well as vitamins and minerals. At least three square meals a day, eight hours of sleep each night, and one to three days off are required to elevate your strength higher than before the workout. Climb too much, sleep too little, skip meals, and eat junk and your abilities will straight-line. Overtraining is the ultimate bad investment because it yields negative returns and frequently leads to injury or sickness.

Nine Absolute Truths and Training Tips

1. The best training for climbing skill (technique and tactics) is climbing.
Always favor climbing as training over nonspecific exercises—such as those at a health club—and time spent during other sports. (See chapter 2 for details.)

2. Climbing skills are specific to the rock type, angle, and frictional properties.
Travel to and pull down on as many different types of rock as possible to expand your library of moves. This will put you on the fast track to 5.12. (See chapter 2 for details.)

3. Skill practice yields a greater return on investment than fitness training for all but elite climbers.
Favor skill practice over strength training at a ratio of three to one. The exception is an elite climber, who will benefit most from a one-to-two ratio of skill practice to strength-training time. (See chapter 2 for details.)

4. General conditioning is the most effective type of fitness training for beginner-level climbers.

Beginner-level climbers should perform mainly general fitness training. Avoid sport-specific exercises during the first few months to a year in this sport. (See chapter 3 for details.)

5. Sport-specific conditioning is the most effective fitness training for advanced climbers.

Advanced climbers must plan and execute an intelligent sport-specific training program to break through plateaus and reach the higher grades. (See chapter 3 for details.)

6. Strength training builds endurance, but endurance training does not build maximum strength.

Focus sport-specific strength training on developing maximum strength over endurance. Climbing a couple of days per week will naturally build endurance. (See chapter 3 for details.)

7. Wasted energy and time are lost forever.

Work for acute awareness of wasted energy and time, whether in the gym or on the rock. Honing your technical and mental skills will yield a windfall of newfound apparent strength as a result of improved economy of movement and decreased emotional energy drain. (See chapters 2 and 4 for details.)

8. Your body cannot go where the mind has not gone first.

Practice visualization daily in a wide variety of everyday activities. In climbing, use visualization when working on new moves, before every climb, in competition, and even while training. This enhances learning and the likelihood of a successful outcome. (See chapter 4 for details.)

9. Training and climbing provide stimulus for, but no actual, muscular growth. Recomposition and strengthening occur only during sleep and on rest days.

Place as high a value on rest time and quality nutrition as you do on training and climbing time. Increase rest volume in proportion to intensity and severity of your training and climbing. (See chapter 3 for details.)

Pushing mental limits is as important as increasing physical capability. Chris Sharma is a pro at doing both. Sharma climbing to first place at the 1999 X Games in San Francisco, California. PHOTO: STEWART GREEN

Evaluating Your Current Performance

Your quest for 5.12 must incorporate constant evaluations and reevaluations to determine your climbing-related strengths, weaknesses, and desires. Strengths are easy to sort out because it's human nature to think about and practice the things at which you are good. Unfortunately, identifying your weaknesses is quite difficult and might not be your idea of a good time. It is necessary, though, if you want to keep your performance curve rising toward 5.12.

A friend's or instructor's objective evaluation is a great place to start—he or she may be able to identify obvious flaws in technique, tactics, and the like. For example, feet scraping at or popping off footholds signals lack of attention to footwork, and constant stretching for holds out of reach is a sign of missed intermediate hand- or footholds and bad sequencing.

A top all-around climber like Roxanna Brock knows the importance of constant self-evaluation and practicing all forms of climbing. Here she's floating up Le Teton (5.9+), Shawangunks, New York.
PHOTO: MIKE LANDKROON

Some fundamental mistakes and weaknesses are subtle, however, and not easily observed. Things such as overgripping holds, holding your breath, high anxiety, poor visualization, and inability to quickly figure out sequences are difficult to diagnose from the ground. A detailed self-assessment is the ticket here. Self-assessment takes the white light of your climbing performance and breaks it into a spectrum of colors representing specific skills. It highlights your strengths and weaknesses and may reveal your hidden Achilles' heel. Only then can you develop a strategic plan for achieving peak performance.

Take the Self-Assessment Test that follows. Read each question once and immediately answer it based on your recent experiences on the rock. Don't read anything into the questions or try to figure out its focus or the "best" answer. When totaling your scores, you'll see that each question focuses on either mental, technical/tactical, or physical skills. A perfect score would be 25 points in all three areas of focus. Keep in mind, however, that the goal of this assessment is to identify weaknesses. It's the low-scoring questions and focus area we are most interested in, because they hold the keys to unlocking higher levels of performance.

Finally, I urge you not to compare your score with anyone else's. Such a comparison is meaningless, since we all hold ourselves to a different standard when taking such self-analysis tests.

Exercise: Self-Assessment Test

Score yourself between 1 and 5 on the following questions. Use the following key for your responses:

1 = almost always
2 = often
3 = sometimes
4 = seldom
5 = never

1. I get anxious and tight as I head into crux sequences.

1   2   3   4   5

2. I miss hidden holds.

1   2   3   4   5

3. I have difficulty hanging on small, necessary-to-use holds.

1   2   3   4   5

4. I make excuses for why I might fail on a route before I even begin to climb.

1   2   3   4   5

5. My forearms balloon and my grip begins to fail even on routes that are easy for me.

1   2   3   4   5

6. On hard sequences, I have difficulty stepping onto critical footholds.

1   2   3   4   5

7. My footwork (use of feet) deteriorates during the hardest part of a climb.

1   2   3   4   5

8. I pump out on overhanging climbs no matter how big the holds.

1   2   3   4   5

9. I train or climb (or do a combination) three days in a row.

    1   2   3   4   5

10. I grab quick draws, the rope, or other gear instead of risking a fall trying a hard move of which I am unsure.

    1   2   3   4   5

11. I have difficulty reading sequences.

    1   2   3   4   5

12. I experience shoulder, elbow, or finger pain when I climb.

    1   2   3   4   5

13. I have more difficulty climbing when people are watching.

    1   2   3   4   5

14. My feet unexpectedly pop off footholds.

    1   2   3   4   5

15. I have difficulty hanging on to small sloping holds or pockets.

    1   2   3   4   5

Calculate your score in the three focus areas.

Mental Questions	Technical Questions	Physical Questions
Q1: _____	Q2: _____	Q3: _____
Q4: _____	Q5: _____	Q6: _____
Q7: _____	Q8: _____	Q9: _____
Q10: _____	Q11: _____	Q12: _____
Q13: _____	Q14: _____	Q15: _____
Total: _____	Total: _____	Total: _____

1. **Slow, deep breathing is the first step to reduce tension and anxiety.**

   Before starting a climb, close your eyes and take five deep belly breaths, each taking about ten seconds. Try to maintain steady breathing as you climb. Take three more slow, deep breaths at each rest position and before the crux sequence. Learn the ANSWER *Sequence for use at each rest position. (See chapter 4.)*

2. **Tunnel vision is a common cause of failure, especially during on-sight climbing.**

   Always completely scope a route before you leave the ground—view the route from a few different positions. As you climb, keep an open mind for hidden holds that may take a little extra effort to find. Chances are there is a good hand- or foothold escaping your view. (See chapter 5.)

3. **Although poor body positioning can make small holds even harder to use, it is likely that you need to increase your maximum grip strength.**

   Spend more time training on steep walls and gym "cave" areas, and go bouldering more often. If you are a more advanced climber, begin using Hypergravity Isolation Training (HIT) as part of your training cycle. If a climbing wall is not available, I recommend performing some hypergravity training twice per week on a fingerboard. (See chapter 3.)

4. **Belief gives birth to reality. If the thought of falling crosses your mind, you likely will.**

   Before you start up a climb, always visualize and feel yourself climbing the route successfully from bottom to top. (See chapter 4.)

5. **You are probably overgripping the holds and/or climbing too slowly.**

   On near-vertical walls relax your grip and place maximum weight on your feet—think about feeling your feet on the holds. When the wall angle becomes overhanging, the number one rule is "climb fast!" (See chapter 2.)

6. **Lack of flexibility is likely your problem.**

   Begin daily stretching for a minimum of ten minutes and practice exaggerated high-stepping on submaximal routes. (See chapter 3.)

7. **You may be focusing on the lack of good handholds instead of zeroing in on crucial footholds (often the key to unlocking hard sequences).**

   When the going gets tough, renew focus on your feet. (See chapters 2 and 5.)

8. On overhanging walls the "pump clock" starts running when you leave the ground. You may not be too weak to do the climb—just too slow!

   Practice climbing at a faster than normal pace on known routes, and look for creative rests that will stop the clock for a few moments. (See chapters 2 and 5.)

9. This is a major error in training strategy that will eventually produce negative results because of overtraining and/or injury.

   Never train three days in a row! Although genetically gifted climbers may get away with it, I do not advise climbers—even advanced individuals—to climb on three consecutive days. (See chapter 3.)

10. Assuming the potential fall is safe, always go for the move instead of grabbing gear or hanging on the rope. The bad habit of grabbing gear is easy to develop and difficult to break. Plus, you'll never learn where your true limit is if you quit or cheat this way.

    Counter any thought of grabbing gear with a targeted focus on the next hold or rest position. (See chapter 4.)

11. Reading sequences comes from experience.

    Climb up to four days a week. Do more on-sight climbing and always try to figure sequences from the ground before you attempt them for real. Put your visualization skills to work. (See chapter 5.)

12. There are two types of elbow tendinitis common to climbers—medial epicondylitis (inside elbow pain) and lateral epicondylitis (outside elbow pain). If you climb long enough, chances are good you'll experience one of them.

    Reverse wrist curls and hand pronators will help prevent these problems. Begin each workout with a single warm-up set of hand pronators and reverse wrist curls, and perform two more sets of each exercise at the end of your workout. (See chapter 3.)

13. Performing under unreasonable pressure is no fun, and the outcome is often less than ideal. The worst (and most common) pressure is the need to perform for others. This is unreasonable and must be shed.

    Climb for your own enjoyment and forget the rest of the world. Relax, get centered, have fun! (See chapter 4.)

14. Popping feet is a common problem even among some advanced climbers. It can also result from too much climbing indoors (where the footholds are more obvious).

Refocus your attention on your feet for a few weeks. Do you carefully place your feet on the best part of a hold or do you simply drop them onto the biggest-looking part? Also, do you hold your foot position stationary as you stand up on that leg? Start downclimbing routes to force your concentration down to your feet. Strive to always feel your feet as you climb. (See chapter 2.)

15. **Open-hand grip strength is crucial. Expert climbers often favor it; beginner climbers avoid it—until they practice with this grip and find how useful it is!**

Begin training and climbing with the open-hand grip. Try to do whole boulder problems, traverses, or routes using only this grip. Employ HIT workouts to increase open-hand maximal strength most rapidly. (See chapter 3.)

Climber on Face Value (5.9), Helen's
Dome, South Platte, Colorado.
PHOTO: STEWART GREEN

CHAPTER TWO

Honing Your Skills — Fast!

If there is any secret at all [to the extraordinary success of French climbers], perhaps it is that we strive for grace, control and fluidity in movement.
—François Legrand

There are several elements to climbing skill, including moves, body positions, tactics, and strategy. Since the playing field always changes, you need to become proficient at what seems to be thousands of variations on each of these elements. The range and complexity of motor learning in climbing is evident in the fact that an advanced climber with twenty years of experience can continue to learn new skills!

Your challenge is to maximize learning of climbing skills in every possible way. This immediately rules out the trial-and-error approach, which is just too slow if you are serious and passionate about this sport. Instead you need to embrace and aggressively utilize specific motor learning techniques. In doing so you will ensure constant, noticeable improvements on the rock.

In this chapter I have outlined sixteen such techniques and rules through which you can accelerate learning of climbing skill and maximize your ability. Understand them, believe in them, and use them!

The Optimal Amount of Climb Time

I'm frequently asked what is the ideal number of climbing days per week to maximize rate of improvement. Unfortunately, a single answer is impossible because it depends on many variables, including skill level, type of climbing, strenuousness of the climbing workout, genetics, and quality of rest. Out of all these variables, the one that weighs most heavily is strenuousness of the climbing workout. There's a strong inverse relationship between the optimal number of climbing days and the strenuousness of the climbing. Interestingly, this goes against conventional wisdom, which says that the stronger athlete performing more strenuous training can climb more. As usual, conventional wisdom is wrong!

Here's the scoop. A novice climber dedicated to learning the fundamental skills on nonstrenuous terrain (for example, slab climbing or low-intensity vertical) can climb just about daily. As improvement takes place, the climber will begin work on steeper, longer, and more strenuous routes. Due to the inverse relationship, such higher-intensity climbing means that fewer climbing days (and more rest days) are optimal. In this common scenario two to four days a week of climbing is ideal.

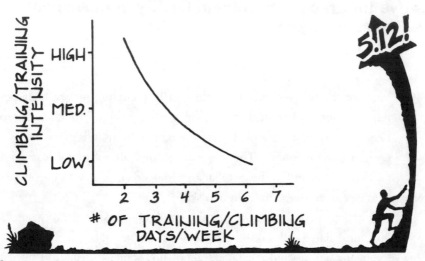

The more strenuous the workout or climbing, the less frequently it should be performed.

The optimal length of a climbing workout is another difficult issue. The standard approach is to climb until completely fatigued. Research has shown that this conventional approach is also flawed. Excessively long practice sessions of complex skills produce poor results, even for motor skills such as golf range practice or shooting practice in basketball where physical fatigue is not a problem. Studies indicate that it's best to keep actual practice time (in this case combined minutes of climbing) under two hours. In fact, half this amount seems to be optimal. About a dozen five-minute routes in the gym seems like a good amount for practice of climbing skills.

Tip: Optimal, not maximal, practice produces the greatest gains in skill. Try for one hour of actual climbing time during each workout. Plan a total of three to five climbing and training days per week, depending on the degree of strenuousness—the more strenuous the workout, the less frequently it should be done.

Practice Days Versus Performance Days

The difference between practice days and performance days lies in the desired outcome. Practice days are for maximal improvement of climbing skills with little concern for performance outcome. Performance days are simply about sending routes and winning comps with no focus on learning or practicing specific climbing skills.

With the exception of elite climbers, practice days should rule. On these days you are free to work on new moves, experiment to find clever rest positions, and try new tactics and strategies, all without any concern or pressure not to fall. This curious and carefree approach will yield steady gains and an occasional major breakthrough!

Unfortunately, many climbers are plagued by the need to perform all the time. Not wanting to make a mistake and fall, they climb tentatively and are gun-shy about trying chancy moves. Even worse, as insurance for good performances, they do the same routes at the same areas or overdose on the local gym. This approach guarantees long-term mediocrity.

Elite climbers are a different breed. With highly honed technical skills and fewer inhibitions, they generally don't hesitate on new moves and have little regard for the pressures of performance. In fact, performance days are their bread and butter. A heavy focus on outcome-based performance will train the few critical skills they may still be lacking: tactics, strategy, and the mental game. Plus, after years of hard work honing the zillions of basic skills, now's their time to bag some savage routes and win a big comp. Besides, nothing beats trial by fire for training elites in any sport.

Tip: Practice days have a greater training value than performance days for all but elite climbers. Each day you train or climb, predetermine whether the goal is practice or performance. Shoot for a three-to-one ratio of practice to performance time.

Learning New Skills

Your body learns and remembers new climbing movements by building detailed "motor performance maps" or schemas in the nervous system and brain. (Some literature, mainly European, uses the term *engram* to describe these motor skills. In keeping with the American scientific literature, I use *schemas* throughout this text.) New schemas are best developed during the early portion of your workout while

Toprope climbing is a great way to learn new moves or practice difficult sequences. This toprope climb is on the A.R.T. Wall at Cliffhangers, Reading, Pennsylvania.

you are fresh to try unknown or difficult movements. Increasing fatigue, a flash pump, even fearful situations mean slow, maybe even no, learning of new climbing skills.

After a complete warm-up, proceed straight into your skill-training problems or routes—now's the time to add to your schema library! This may not be the most physical part of your session, but it can be the most productive if it's heavily focused on new or problem techniques, moves, or situations. Whether it's delicate face climbing, drop knees on overhanging rock, or thin handcrack technique, jump on it fresh.

A safe, fear-free environment is also a big help at learning new moves fast. Indoor walls win the prize here because of their convenience and comfort. But get outside as much as possible, because no gym can match the variety of moves available on real rock. Either way, start off working your most uncomfortable skills or type of terrain while you're fresh.

Tip: Practice of new skills is most effective when you're well rested, fully warmed up, and in a safe environment. Use the thirty minutes immediately following your warm-up to practice new moves, techniques, and weak skill areas. Indoor walls, topropes, and boulders are the ideal forum.

Blocked Practice of Difficult Moves

"Blocked" practice (identical repetitions of a move) is the most popular method of training hard climbing skills, whether at the gym or crag. Misuse of blocked practice is common among climbers, however, and can have negative effects on performance. Let's sort things out.

Blocked, repetitive practice of new skills will produce rapid positive results. For instance, when learning a difficult boulder problem, you perform repeated attempts of the exact desired sequence. Or suppose you want to learn finger-jamming technique: The focus is laps on fingercracks for a session or two. These are both appropriate uses of blocked practice.

Upon development of feel and confidence and some rate of success at the new task, a radical change is needed. Further blocked reps have little value and may even result in a false sense of confidence and poor use of the skill in settings different from that practiced. An example would be a climber who has wired a route at his or her home crag through countless ascents but can't send similar routes on a road trip. The same phenomenon is seen in other sports, like a golfer who hits perfectly during regular practices at the range (blocked) but is in the trees, sand, and water during rare visits to a course.

These examples show that after the first few successful trials of a task, blocked practice is for blockheads! Beyond this point, additional gains require variable and randomized practice.

Tip: Use blocked practice to accelerate learning during the initial trials of a new move, skill, or sequence. After two or three successful repetitions, cease blocked practice in favor of variable and randomized practice.

Variable Practice of Skills

It's not enough to acquire use of a move or skill in a single setting. The ultimate goal is instant and proficient use of the skill in any novel situation you come upon. The tried and proven way to do this is with variable practice.

Suppose you've just learned the drop-knee move on a vertical indoor wall with large, positive holds. To incorporate variable practice you would now

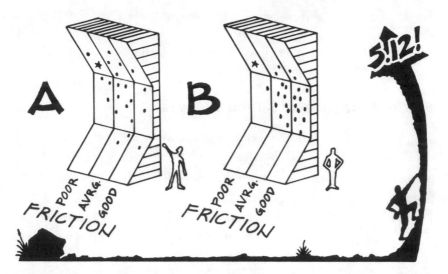

Climber A has developed more diverse schemas (dots) and thus will be able to closely approximate the novel move (star)—possibly on-sight it! Climber B's more limited schemas will have him flailing and probably failing on the novel move (star).

change the route conditions slightly and attempt the same drop-knee move again. After a few reps in this situation, change the conditions even more.

Indoor walls are ideal for variable practice sessions. Do the desired move one way, then change the hold size and try it again. Adjust the spacing of the holds and attempt another rep. Finally, switch to another section of wall and perform the move at a different angle. Change the conditions every few trials whether you succeed or not, to prevent blocking of the practice.

Now the exciting part: Variable practice of a move over several workouts will develop solid schemas relating to use of the move over a wide range of conditions (angle, hold size, rock type, and friction properties). Such schemas enable you to perform moves in novel situations on-sight, even if you've never done that exact move in practice! Elite climbers often comment after sending a route on-sight that the right moves and body positions "came to them intuitively." They have their schemas to thank for the success.

Tip: Variable practice expands the learning of newly acquired skills for use over a wide range of conditions (angle, hold size, rock type, and so forth). Use this drill regularly, always varying the route conditions more than you expect they'll ever occur on a real-world route. Change the conditions every few attempts to avoid blocked practice.

Variable practice of moves develops solid schemas. Here Scott Meckler demonstrates how you can practice a backstep move in six increasingly difficult situations.

1. Initial learning of the backstep move in an easy vertical setting.

2. The same move is practiced on a slightly overhanging wall.

3. Further practice on smaller holds on a slightly overhanging wall.

4. Backstep move practiced on a steeper wall with large holds.

5. A more difficult back-step move with tiny footholds and a small undercling handhold.

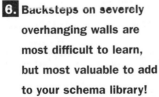

6. Backsteps on severely overhanging walls are most difficult to learn, but most valuable to add to your schema library!

Physical guidance aids learning of difficult or strenuous moves. A good spotter both protects against dangerous falls and is ready to lend some physical aid when learning a difficult move.

Skill Guidance Methods

The main methods of skill guidance in climbing are verbal help in solving a sequence and physical aid in executing a move. Although both are effective in facilitating learning, misuse can produce long-term negative effects. Verbal description of moves and sequences is invaluable during early stages of learning. Such spoon-fed instruction accelerates learning by shortcutting the slower trial-and-error approach. This is completely appropriate for a novice climber.

Unfortunately, excessive beta (as it's commonly called) beyond the earliest stages of learning can interfere with the development of problem-solving skills, inhibit learning of complex movements, and ultimately degrade your climbing potential. Research clearly shows that even moderate amounts of verbal guidance yield poor performances when the guidance is removed. Thus if your goal is simply to get up a route (redpoint) as fast as possible, maximum verbal guidance will aid your performance. On the other hand, if your long-term goal is a broad proficiency in this sport with maximum on-sight and competitive skills, beta is a handicap that will hold you back.

The second type of guidance is physical help through a move, via a yank on the rope or a push on the bum. Once again, such guidance is an excellent aid in learning a new skill when used sparingly. Physical aids are best used in bouldering where just a light touch is enough to coax you through a move. More invasive physical aids such as getting hauled through a sequence by your belayer or pushed into an awkward position by your spotter have minimal benefits.

Tip: Use skill guidance to accelerate learning of moves and sequences. Ask (demand) verbal and physical aid when attempting a new skill or in search of a quick ascent. Avoid excessive skill guidance (especially beta), however, which will produce long-term negative results. Don't hesitate to shout off beta and figure out the move yourself!

Self-Awareness of Performance

Keen self-awareness is crucial for optimal climbing performance. In the context of this chapter, your task is to monitor your climbing technique and efficiency of movement. Ultimately, it's the aggregate of minor inefficiencies and slight flaws in technique that brings a climber down short of reaching the summit. The evidence is played out at gyms and crags across the country. We've all seen and experienced it. It goes like this.

A group of climbers are working a route whose crux sequence has one best solution. Each climber attempts the same sequence, but only one person succeeds. Why does the sequence work for one person but not the others? In many cases the answer lies in a number of minor technical flaws that are unknowingly sabotaging performances. These flaws may range from climbing too slowly, to undue tension in antagonistic muscles, to sloppy placements of the feet, to over-gripping of holds, to mental miscues. The key to nixing these problems is self-awareness—never-ending checks and rechecks of the goings-on in your mind and body, followed by tiny adjustments. Elite climbers probably do this hundreds of times during a single ascent (often unknowingly!). Beginners, on the other hand, may never do it because they are overwhelmed by the immediate concern of solving the next move.

Make a conscious effort to develop this skill early on in your climbing career. It will enhance your performance and help in identification and elimination of bad habits. Remember, just as climbing skills become hardwired after a few repetitions, so do bad habits such as overgripping and sloppy feet.

Tip: Constant self-awareness is essential for improving poor skills, eliminating bad habits, and increasing performance quality. Ask yourself questions to increase this awareness. For example, "Is this the best body position? Am I using proper footwork and minimal upper-body strength? Am I climbing at the best pace?"

Modeling Advanced Climbers

One type of guidance you can never overdose on is modeling of advanced climbers. Whether in business or sports, modeling someone successful is one of the surest ways to find out what works.

Modeling is best used in a climbing gym, where you can observe the movements, positions, and techniques of advanced climbers, then give them a try on your own. Make a mental picture of what you want to attempt and use that vision as a starting point. Experiment, modify, and make the move your own. Who knows—you just might find a better way of doing it!

You can also model what you observe at the crags. In addition to actual moves, take special note of the tactics and strategy used by high-end climbers. For example, how do they work crux sequences? Where do they find rests? At what pace do they climb? How do they go about equipping routes? Again, it's best to first experiment with your observations in the gym before you test them outdoors.

Although modeling technical skills is a powerful weapon for your arsenal, copying an elite climber's fitness training can easily backfire. Remember that elite climbers have spent years conditioning their muscles and tendons to withstand extreme levels of stress. To train as they do without this long-term preparation could be disastrous.

Tip: Modeling the techniques and tactics (not training) of advanced climbers is a powerful learning tool. Begin to spend as much time observing other climbers as you do actually climbing. Take note of new moves, rest positions, tactics, and such, and experiment with them on your own. The images you pick up are the seeds of future advancements.

Developing a Broad Repertoire of Skills

One of the oldest principles in the field of motor learning and performance is that "transfer of learning between two tasks increases as the similarity between them increases." This explains why proficiency in one type of climbing does not guarantee success in any other. We've all seen climbers who excel in just one

Modeling advanced climbers' techniques, tactics, and movements is an excellent method of learning. Here Bobbi Bensman executes a great clipping position—straight arm with weight in over the feet—on Vitamin H (5.12c/d), Rifle, Colorado.

PHOTO: STEWART GREEN

style (for example, traditional) or at one angle (for example, steep sport routes), or even in one geographic area; it's quite rare, however, to find a person who's brilliant across the board. Here's why.

Suppose you spend most of your time climbing artificial walls. You'll certainly get good at climbing said terrain, but venture outdoors and you'll be in for a good spanking. Or what if you specialize in crack climbing? Although you may become a stonemaster of Valley cracks, an attempt on a Rifle sport route would have the fat lady singing by the second bolt.

Michael Jordan proved that basketball-throwing skills do not transfer well to baseball-throwing skills. So don't expect indoor climbing skills to transfer outdoors or for face-climbing skills to transfer to cracks. To become a great climber, you need to log extensive, wide-ranging practice. Real rock is the ticket here, and the more you travel to different areas, the better. You'll develop a broad set of schemas and ultimately perform well in any situation.

Thus, although specializing in one type of climbing (say, sport climbing) will yield the most rapid short-term gains, such blocked practice will limit your potential in all other areas. Conversely, long-term exposure to many types of climbing can enhance performance in your specialty area. For instance, sport climbers can use crack techniques such as hand and knee jams for a vital rest—that is, if they know the technique!

Tip: Climbing on a wide variety of rock is the single most important element of skill training. Get outdoors and travel as much as possible to develop a wide repertoire of techniques, tactics, and moves. Avoid specialization—it will limit your long-term potential.

On-Sight Practice Payoffs

Climbing is a complex game of problem solving, strategy, movement, and mental fortitude. You will never realize your true potential unless you work consistently on all these areas. On-sight climbing is the most powerful means of developing these skills in proportion to one another.

On-sighting is defined as "climbing with zero prior knowledge, information, or clues of any kind." Thus on-sighting a chalked sport route or tagged indoor climb is a somewhat diluted form of on-sight. This fine point aside, heading up on any kind of climb with the burden of deciphering it yourself holds great practice value. The purer the on-sight, the greater the value, of course.

As discussed earlier, verbal guidance (beta) is useful only in the formative stages of learning. To the intermediate or advanced climber, beta yields only short-term gratification with no long-term benefits. It's as if Bobby Fischer spoon-fed every move to you during a chess match you were playing. You'd surely win the match but gain no skill as his pawn (pun intended).

Tip: On-sight climbing develops the widest range of technical and cognitive skills. Climb on-sight weekly, whether at the gym or crags. It's like taking skill-building steroids—but these side effects are good for you!

The Synergy of Mental and Physical Practice

Interlacing mental and physical practice undoubtedly yields faster learning of sport skills than either alone. If you are not employing mental practice between every climbing rep and during rest days, you are surely giving up a major edge. Use of mental imagery can range from simply visualizing a move before you try it to running a detailed mental movie of a long, sequential climb prior to a red-point. Repeat the visualization often, making the images as accurate, detailed, and vivid as possible. This will provide best results.

As with physical skills, your mental abilities will improve with practice. Always climb each sequence or route at least once mentally before attempting it. Sure, it takes extra effort and time to exercise your imagination in this way, but the payoffs are very real! It's a safe bet that not a single Olympic athlete gives away this powerful edge, so why should you?

Tip: Interlacing mental and physical practice of skills produces greater results than physical practice alone. Visualizing a new move or sequence at least once before each attempt will enhance learning and increase the odds of success. Employ regular mental practice during rest periods (or days) to build confidence and further code known sequences.

Speed Training of Skills

One of the most ignored yet important climbing skills is climbing fast. No, not speed climbing as in the competitions, but faster-than-normal movement (for you) through hard sequences without loss of technique. This is fundamental for conserving energy on difficult routes, but it takes practice.

Known or "wired" routes at the gym or local crag are ideal to begin training this skill. Since you already know the moves, you can move briskly through difficult sections with little thought. Concentrate on climbing quickly from one rest position to the next. Your goal is not to race to the top with sloppy, inefficient moves, but instead to climb as fast as possible while maintaining perfect technique.

**Mia Axon on Kiss The Cobble
(5.13b), Maple Canyon, Utah.**

PHOTO: STEWART GREEN

Slow down at the first sign you're making errors, whether it's a foot pop or botched sequence. Climbing fast in poor form has no value.

You may want to occasionally experiment with accelerated on-sight climbing since most climbers tend to climb too slowly in this setting. Pick a lengthy toprope climb at the gym or a well-bolted sport climb so safety is not a concern. Scope the route extensively and visualize as many of the moves as you can from the ground. When you are relaxed and ready, attack the route with a vengeance and don't worry about the outcome. Remember, this is practice.

After a few months, you will find yourself climbing faster on all routes, on-sight or not. This drill will clear up your misconceptions about the right speed to climb on different types of routes. Your efficacy will skyrocket thanks to heightened awareness of the relationship between speed and fatigue.

Tip: Performing known sequences and routes at accelerated speed increases long-term proficiency. Use speed climbing at least once a week to stretch the bonds of where you can climb both quickly and accurately.

Downclimbing Routes

Every time you lower off the top of a climb, you miss out on one of the most effective training exercises: downclimbing. That's right—if you really want to get better in this sport, and fast, then rechalk at the top of a route and begin climbing back down.

Downclimbing improves many skills, including footwork, sense of body positioning, speed of movement, hold recognition, and sequence memory, to name a few. It's also great fitness training since you're increasing the length of your "burn" and performing eccentric muscle movements. All totaled, this makes downclimbing a hands-down must on all but performance days.

Clearly, toprope setups facilitate more carefree, go-for-it attempts at downclimbing a route. Whether at the gym or a crag, find a good belayer who can pay out rope at just the right rate—you don't want to get hung up by the rope while reversing the crux sequence! Continue downclimbing until muscular failure hits or you botch a sequence and fall. Whether you get back on and continue or lower to the ground (on a steep route you may have no choice) is up to you. Do be careful not to go overboard on this training method. If you fall more than a few times while downclimbing, call it quits and move on to the next (up) climb.

I cautiously advise downclimbing of lead routes. Overhanging sport routes are the best choice here; in fact, downclimbing is a nice alternative to untying and threading anchors. A veteran belayer is mandatory, however, especially as you enter the ground-out zone near the last (lower) two bolts.

Tip: Downclimbing routes is a powerful skill-training exercise. Don't overlook this method of training the triad of skill, fitness, and mental abilities. On practice days downclimb every route you send as far as possible.

Fatigued Skill Practice

Earlier I pointed out that it's best to practice new skills while you're fresh. Interestingly, you can increase your command of known skills through practice during states of moderate fatigue. This is a powerful concept you'll want to put to work immediately—but be careful not to misuse it.

Research has shown that beyond the initial successful trials of a skill, practice should be performed with variable conditions and levels of fatigue. This will increase your rate of failure at doing certain moves, but performance isn't your goal, practice is! The benefits of this practice, no matter how poor, will become evident in the future. Besides, this concept actually makes good sense. If you want the ability to stick a deadpoint in the midst of a dicey lead climb while pumped, you'd better log some deadpoints in various states of fatigue during practice.

Here's the best approach. Use the first thirty minutes of your workout (while fresh) to train new skills, then move on to chalking up some mileage on a variety of routes. After an hour or so, or when moderately fatigued, attempt several reps of recently acquired moves or sequences. As fatigue increases, finish up with some reps of sequences or boulder problems you have more completely mastered.

In the context of a two-hour climbing-gym workout, this rule emphasizes the benefit of squeezing in a greater volume of climbing with only brief rests over doing just a few performance reps with extensive rest. The long rests and performance climbing may make you *look* better, but the greater volume of practice will make you *climb* better!

Finally, don't confuse practice while muscularly fatigued with practice while tired or injured. As with any training method, you can go overboard and end up getting negative results. Sixty to ninety minutes of actual climbing time is optimal.

Tip: Practice recently acquired skills while moderately fatigued to increase your mastery of them and to build long-term retention. Attempting well-known skills and sequences during higher levels of fatigue is likewise beneficial.

"Send me" is an excellent method of random skill practice.

Random Skill Practice

The ability to on-sight a sequence of novel moves on foreign rock is the ultimate goal of your skill practice time. Toward this end, the best workout approach (after practicing new skills while fresh) is a randomized free-for-all of skill types. This highly effective method is widely used in other sports and should not be overlooked by climbers as top training for the unknown.

There are two approaches to random training of climbing skills. First, on an indoor wall attempt to link a sequence of very different bouldering moves. Put your right brain to work on contriving a bizarre (not hard), random sequence of moves. Take several tries at sending it. Better yet, team up with your most deranged friend on a round of the stick game (aka "send me"). Take turns pointing (with a broomstick) each other through a perverse sequence of movements. The ideal route is an unlikely, random selection of moderately difficult moves.

The second, more powerful method of randomization training is to climb a series of widely differing routes in rapid succession. A commercial gym with many different angles, a few cracks, and a roof or two is ideal. Team with a partner and toprope five to ten routes of different character within an hour. The first route may be a vertical face, the next a slab, the third a fingercrack, the fourth an overhanging pumpfest, the fifth a handcrack, the sixth a roof route, and so forth. This rapid recall of a wide range of techniques is skill training at its best.

You can use both of these random practice methods outdoors as well. The advantage of real rock is a wider range of route and move types; the downside is that it takes longer to locate and set up appropriate routes.

Tip: Random practice of known skills enhances functional use and long-term recall. Do a random skill workout at least once a week. Use as wide a range of moves and route types as possible to maximize effectiveness.

Feedback and Video Analysis

The best climbers seem to have no obvious weak areas. They perform well in just about any setting, anytime. This is largely due to their understanding and use of many of the aforementioned skill-training methods. But it's their relentless pursuit of identifying and fixing weak areas, with the goal of perfection, that separates the best from the rest.

It begins with day-to-day self-awareness and self-analysis of every aspect of your practice and performance. But it can't stop there; some problems require an objective point of view to be fully revealed. For starters, an instructor, a coach, or even your partner can provide verbal feedback and guidance as you climb. This guidance should be focused on pointing out poor technique or tactics, not on giving beta.

Another popular method of feedback in sports is videotape. Have a friend (not your belayer) videotape you climbing several different types of routes. If possible, get some footage both indoors and out and on toprope and lead. View the tape straight through, noting differences in your style, control, attack, and emotions from one route type to the next and between toprope and lead. This evaluation alone should provide tons of feedback on your general strengths and weaknesses.

Next, dissect each climb in detail with liberal use of rewind and slow-motion play. Take note of even the most minor problems—whether bent arms in a rest position, scraping feet in the midst of a crux, tight slow movements, lack of decisiveness and go-for-it, or whatever.

After reviewing a route on tape and noting errors, visualize the desired corrections to each problem. Make a mental movie with all the right moves spliced in place of the outtakes. When feasible, return to the climb and attempt the corrections you've envisioned.

The power of videotape in enhancing performance cannot be overstated. All types of performers, from network newscasters to professional football players, spend hours each week reviewing footage in search of even the smallest glitch in performance. I challenge you to commit a minimum of two hours per month to video analysis. It's invaluable, and it's a blast!

Tip: Get frequent feedback from your partner, a coach, or a more advanced climber. Better yet, use video analysis to critique yourself and identify your weaknesses du jour. Make written notes of what you observe, then use visualization to build a blueprint of an alternate, correct reality you'll execute on the rock.

Eric Scully on Hunchback Arête (5.11a), Mount Lemmon, Arizona. PHOTO: STEWART GREEN

CHAPTER THREE

Welcome to Conditioning

The hardest part of training is making the decision to start at all. —Wolfgang Güllich

The desire for greater strength is inherent in most athletes—and climbers are no exception. Increased strength is handy as you crank increasingly hideous routes on your trip toward 5.12 (and, of course, beyond). Getting honed and buffed also helps you with the head games: More strength breeds confidence, and greater confidence breeds success.

Unfortunately, too many climbers obsess on strength training prior to perfecting the fundamentals of climbing movement. This approach will stunt technical growth, increase frustrations, and ultimately reduce the chances of attaining the skill and strength to become a true master of rock. So whether your long-term goal is to boulder V10, win a PCA comp, or just climb 5.10 someday, exercise your patience and put first things first. Dialing in technique and tactics must be the top priority, while maximizing strength is far in second place.

This chapter provides a streamlined three-part discussion on getting fit for the rocks. Let's begin by examining the basic elements of physical conditioning for beginner- to intermediate-level climbers. Next is a cutting-edge, to-the-point look into sport-specific strength training for more advanced climbers. The chapter concludes with details on preventing injury and speeding recovery through proper nutrition and rest.

Keep in mind that this chapter is not a comprehensive text on strength training. Consult *Training for Climbing* for a broader discussion of this topic, and visit my TrainingForClimbing.com Web site for the very latest information.

Basic Training Program

Physical fitness is one of the three elements in the climbing performance triad, the others being your technical and mental abilities (see figure below). While climbing will yield positive results in all three areas, pure fitness training will only make you more fit. Thus, as Absolute 3 (chapter 1) points out, most of us will cash in a greater return in performance from time invested climbing than in fitness training.

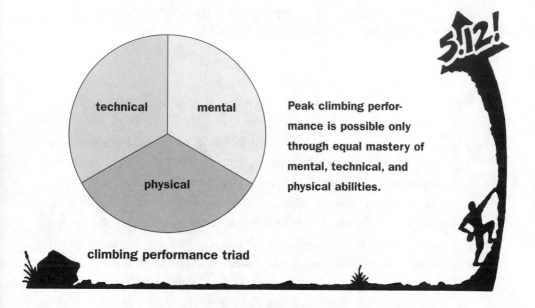

Peak climbing performance is possible only through equal mastery of mental, technical, and physical abilities.

climbing performance triad

What about beginner- to intermediate-level climbers who still want or need to do some fitness training? They should focus on four areas: reducing body weight, increasing flexibility, general muscular conditioning, and improving strength in the pull muscles.

Optimizing Body Composition

If you've ever climbed with a big pack, a heavy rack, or a long, thick rope, you've experienced the negative effects of increased weight on performance. Likewise, reasonable weight loss can have a strong positive effect on your climbing. Your goal is not the anorexic look of an underfed, overtrained climber, but instead a tight V-shaped physique featuring the skinny legs of a distance runner and an upper body somewhat like a gymnast. Prototype physiques that exemplify this look are Chris Sharma, Lisa Rands, and Dean Potter, to name a few.

First, let's state the obvious. Excessive body fat is bad. But so is excessively low body fat, which will leave you weak, slow to recover, and unable to build muscle. The optimal body fat percentage for men is 6 to 12 percent; for women, 8 to 16 percent. If you're not sure how you measure up, consider having your body fat tested. Or you can use the economical "pinch-an-inch" method on your waistline (actually a good gauge). If you can pinch an inch (or more), you are not in the optimal ranges.

For a climber, excessive muscular weight is about as bad as excessive fat. In fact, since muscle weighs more than fat per unit volume, large muscles in the wrong place are worse than fat. As a comparison, imagine Arnold Schwarzenegger and John Goodman sieging a route at Smith Rocks. The results would be hugely negative for both men!

Inappropriate training is the usual cause of unwanted muscle. For instance, the leg exercises performed by bodybuilders or bike racers are a waste of time for climbers since lack of leg strength is rarely the limiting factor on the rock. Bicep curls and heavy bench- and shoulder-press exercises are another example. They will pump you up nicely for the beach but weigh you down on the rock. What is your priority?

There are two common methods of stripping away unwanted fat and muscle that have worked for climbers. First is the low-fat, low-protein, low-calorie diet combined with maximal climbing (a popular method for on-the-road climbers trying to live on a dollar a day). Although initial results may be positive, the long-term effects of consistent undernutrition (lack of calories and protein) include a plateau (or drop) in performance, excessive loss of muscle, sickness, injury, and depression.

A better approach for reaching optimal body weight is a high-quality (not high-calorie) diet and regular aerobic activity. The diet should consist of three squares, with a total macronutrient caloric breakdown of approximately 65 percent carbohydrate, 15 percent protein, and 20 percent fat.

An active male wanting to lose some weight might restrict his total dietary intake to around 2,000 calories per day (25 percent more on extremely active days). This would break down to about 320 grams of carbohydrate, 80 grams of protein, and 45 grams of fat. Similarly, an active female climber hoping to drop a few pounds should get positive results by limiting total daily food consumption to about 1,500 calories (20 percent more on extremely active days). Strive for a macronutrient breakdown of around 240 grams of carbohydrate, 60 grams of protein, and 35 grams of fat. I do not advise long-term caloric restriction below these levels.

Activity-wise, running is most effective for incinerating fat and shrinking unwanted muscle. Don't worry about your climbing muscles, which will be maintained as long as you continue to climb regularly and consume at least 1 gram of protein per kilogram of body weight per day. Other popular aerobic activities such as heavy-duty mountain biking and the StairMaster yield mixed results; they do eat up body fat but may maintain (or build) undesirable leg muscle.

Frequency of aerobic training should be proportionate to your distance from ideal weight. For example, if you are far overweight, then daily twenty- to forty-minute runs are an important part of your training-for-climbing program. As you near ideal weight, one to three twenty-minute runs per week are sufficient. Upon reaching your optimal weight, very little aerobic training is required, since bouldering and cragging require only modest aerobic fitness. Your training time is better invested on sport-specific exercises or climbing.

Flexibility Training

Okay, I admit it. I hate stretching! After all, it's human nature to hate doing things at which we're poor, and my flexibility stinks. Seriously, athletes can't ignore any weaknesses if they want to continue to improve. I have developed the habit of stretching before and after each workout, and I've made some modest improvements to boot. Of course, I realize I'll never be doing disco splits like Tim "TNT" Toula. Flexibility is largely determined by genetics, so my goal is to stretch enough to realize my potential. In doing so, I open up more moves on vertical face climbs, lower the chance of certain injuries, and speed recovery after workouts.

Whether you are gifted in this area or not, there are six basic stretches I consider the minimal requirements. Do them before and after each workout. Consider them mandatory at the start of a day at the crags.

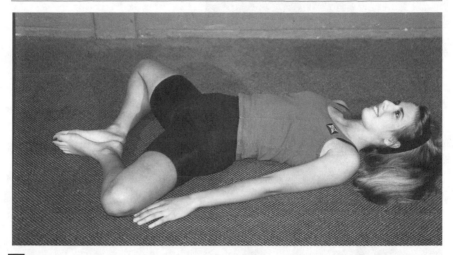

1. **Froggies (aka butterflies).** This stretch works the hip turnout so crucial for climbing near-vertical walls. Lie flat on your back and place the soles of your feet together, with your legs bent about three-quarters of the way. Relax and allow your knees to drop to the side toward the floor. You can increase the stretch by having someone carefully apply pressure onto your knees. Perform five stretches, each lasting twenty to thirty seconds.

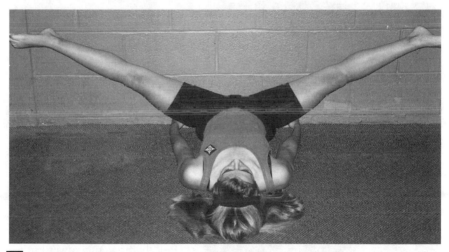

2. **Wall splits.** This is an easy stretch for the groin and legs. Start with your legs elevated and together, with your butt a few inches away from the wall. Slowly separate your legs (heels resting on the wall) until you feel the stretch begin. Keep your lower back to the floor throughout and let gravity pull your legs out (down) to the side. Hold the stretch for two to four minutes.

3. **High steps.** This "active" stretch is the best single exercise to improve the valuable high-step skill. Stand against an unused section of vertical climbing wall with your feet forward and toes touching the wall. Grab two handholds for balance and lift one leg as high as possible to your side as if to step on a hold at hip level (if there's actually a hold there, then place your foot on it!). Repeat this high-step stretch ten times on both sides. Try to step a bit higher each time without moving away from the wall.

4. **Forearm stretches.** Mandatory! While standing, place the fingers of the straight arm (arm to be stretched) into the palm of the opposite hand. Pull back on the fingers and hand of the straight arm until you feel the stretch begin. Hold for ten seconds. Now make a fist and flex the hand in the other direction. Pull the fist gently inward in order to stretch the back of the forearm. Do three sets of these stretches with each forearm, holding each stretch for at least ten seconds.

5. Shoulder and upper back. Pull your elbow across your chest toward the opposite shoulder. While still pulling, slowly move the elbow up and down to work the complete stretch.

6. Upper arm and lat. With arms overhead and bent at the elbows, grab one elbow and pull it behind your head until you feel a stretch in the triceps and shoulder. Finish by slowly leaning sideways in the direction of the stretch to extend it below the shoulder and into the lat muscles. As with previous stretches, remember to work both sides.

Perform a few minutes of light aerobic activity (for example, jogging or jumping rope) before beginning your stretching. After stretching, massage your fingers, hands, and forearms for a few minutes. This practice increases warming blood flow to the connective tissues, tendons, and muscles most stressed while climbing.

Strength Training 101

The importance of muscular strength to climbing performance has probably been obvious since your first pump on the first climb of your first day on the rock. The natural conclusion is to place a high priority on gaining more strength in the forearms, upper arms, and back. Unfortunately, this is the biggest and most common error in training for climbing. An obsession with strength training early on will stunt your technical growth and may handicap your climbing skill for years to come.

Absolute 3 (see chapter 1) emphasizes that gains in performance come more quickly from practice of climbing skills than strength training during the formative years. The good news is that in addition to increasing skill, climbing is also a pretty good muscular workout. It's the two-birds-with-one-stone idea: Climb as a workout and you'll improve both skill and strength. If you go to the health club for a strength workout, you will gain some strength (although it may not be specific to climbing), but you will do nothing to develop skill.

Climbing long routes or lapping short ones trains muscular endurance. Working on crux moves and general bouldering will help build strength. Get on a variety of terrain and literally every muscle from your feet to your forearms will get into the act. Muscular workouts like this are far more useful than doing a circuit of machines at the local health club. Forget the iron. Get climbing!

Supplemental Strength-Training Exercises

Some supplemental strength training is advised if you can't climb three or four days per week. Your workout must be tailored to climbing—a friend's bodybuilding workout won't do. Put some thought into figuring out what exercises are most specific to climbing. The closer the exercise is to the actual climbing positions, the better. For instance, pull-ups are similar to more climbing movements than, say, bicep curls. Fingerboard hangs are specific to how you grip the rock; handheld squeezers are not. A lat pulldown machine at the gym is somewhat specific to climbing; the bench press is not. If you're not sure about an exercise, nix it. And most of all, ignore what the muscleheads are doing.

In addition, favor body-weight exercises such as push-ups and dips over machines or free weights. If you possess ordinary leg strength (for example, you are able to step up stairs two or three at a time), forget any strength training for the legs. Keep the weights light (between 50 and 75 percent of body weight) when using free weights and machines. The exceptions are pulldown exercises, which you can work at body weight or higher. High resistances build bigger muscles, and the pullers are the only place this is acceptable.

1. Pull-ups. This most obvious exercise for climbers is useful for beginners but hardly worth the time for elites. Use large holds on a fingerboard or grip a pull-up bar with palms away. Do five sets to failure with a two- to three-minute rest between sets. Three days per week is optimal.

Your long-term goal is five sets of ten to twenty repetitions. When you reach this, begin to add weight around your waist (a 10- or 20-pound weight belt is ideal). Initially, if you can't do five sets of at least six reps (common), employ a spotter to aid you by lifting around your waist. Another option is to work negative reps to complete each set; that is, use a chair to step up to the top position and lower down through the range of motion to a slow five-second count. Either way, it's important to achieve a minimum of six reps.

2. **Uneven-grip pull-ups.** Grip a pull-up bar with one hand while the other hand is holding on to a towel (between 6 and 18 inches lower) looped over the bar. Alternatively, hang a loop of 1-inch webbing over the bar and grip it with two or three fingers. Both hands pull, but the upper hand is emphasized. Do a set to failure, then rest for a minute or two and switch sides. Repeat twice. Increase the vertical distance between hands if you can do eight or more reps. Do this twice a week, and in a few months to a year you'll be close to a one-arm pull-up!

3. **Lat pulldown.** Do this in place of, not in addition to, pull-ups. This is one exercise you can do like the bodybuilders, although your hand spacing should vary only a few inches from shoulder width (if you don't perform uneven-grip pull-ups, then you would benefit from working the lat pulldowns one arm at a time). Use a heavy weight that allows you just six to twelve high-intensity reps. Take a two-minute rest between five total sets. Do these a maximum of two days per week.

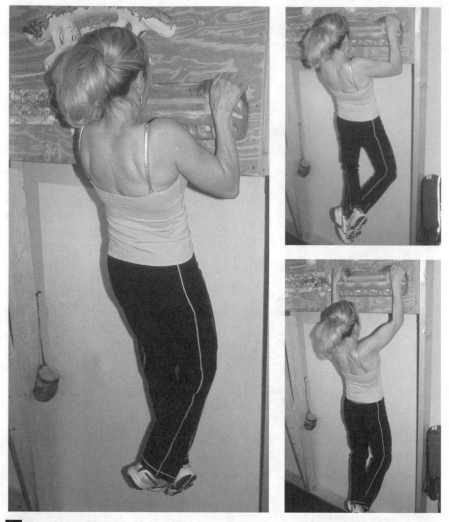

4. Frenchies. These babies will fry your pull muscles. Consider doing three sets one day per week in place of your other pull-muscle exercises. Start at the top position of a pull-up (palms away, hands shoulder width apart) and hold there in a lock-off position for five seconds. Lower to the bottom and pull up to the top again; this time, however, immediately lower halfway (to an arm angle of 90 degrees) and hold a lock-off there for five seconds. Lower to the bottom and do another pull-up, after which you'll lock off at an arm angle of about 120 degrees. Hold for five seconds and lower to the bottom position. Perform this exact sequence and you've completed one full cycle—but keep going if you can! Do as many continuous cycles, or part thereof, until failure. Rest for five minutes between sets. Don't cheat on the five-second counts!

5. **Fingerboard hangs.** Repeaters may be the single best fingerboard regimen, because they will build contact strength in a variety of grips. One set of repeaters involves a series of six maximal-intensity hangs (on the same hold) lasting three to ten seconds each and separated by just a five-second rest. Favor small- to medium-sized edges, pockets, and pinches. Do two consecutive sets on each of six to ten different grips (twelve to twenty total sets). Each set must be maximal intensity, so add weight to your body to ensure failure in ten seconds on each rep. Rest for one minute between sets. Always perform a good warm-up, including a few easy hangs on the holds to be worked. Limit yourself to two repeater workouts per week.

6. **Abdominal crunches and hanging knee lifts.** Perform crunches lying on the floor with your feet and lower legs up on a chair and knees bent at 90 degrees. Cross your arms over your chest and lift your shoulders off the floor or bench. Exhale with each "up" repetition and continue until failure. Rest for one minute between each of three to five total sets.

As you progress to harder and steeper routes, add some hanging knee lifts to your abdominal workout. Hang from a pull-up bar and lift your knees toward your chest. Two sets to failure will hit your abs better than a lifetime of using some bogus TV infomercial ab trainer.

7. **Reverse wrist curls.** Using a 5- to 20-pound dumbbell, perform these wrist curls palm-down and with your forearm resting on your knee, a bench, or a table. Do approximately twenty half repetitions; that is, begin with your hand in the neutral position (straight), then curl it upward until it's fully extended. Do one set as part of your warm-up and two more sets at the end of your workout.

8. Hand pronators. Exercise machines and devices for working hand pronation are a rarity—if you find one, buy it! Otherwise, you can whip up a makeshift pronation trainer in a few minutes. Cut a 12-inch piece of broomstick and mount just a few 1-pound weights securely on one end (actually 1.25-pound York barbell weights are ideal and can be purchased at most sporting goods stores). Hold the free end in the hand to be trained and rotate your hand side to side (thumb turning from three o'clock position to nine o'clock and back). Vary resistance by either adding weight or moving your hand farther down the stick (away from the weighted end).

Basic Training Tips

- Reducing body weight is often the fastest way to increase strength-to-weight ratio. If you are overweight (or overly muscular), make aerobic training and a high-quality diet a priority. Remember, weight loss will yield faster gains in apparent strength than actual strength training. Run up to thirty minutes three to seven days per week. Taper the amount of aerobic activity as you approach optimal body weight.

- Flexibility training aids development of some technical skills and lowers potential for injury. Stretch before and after every workout for at least five to fifteen minutes to enable unhindered movement and speed muscular recovery, respectively.

- Climbing is the best general strength training for climbing. If you climb at least three days per week, there is little need for supplemental strength training during your formative years. Vary the type of climbing to maximize the all-around fitness-training effect.

- Keep supplemental training specific to climbing. Buy a fingerboard or pull-up bar or, better yet, build a home wall. Favor body-weight exercises over machines.

Advanced Training Program

If you've been climbing a few years, can send 5.10 in your sleep, and your technique and tactical skills are up to snuff, you are ready to embark on some serious sport-specific strength training. Still, you must not obsess on this aspect of training at the expense of everything else. Jump into this type of training too early or too fast and it will hurt your technical growth and get you injured. Proceed with caution, and remember that this section is just a primer on the subject—certainly not the final word.

Sport-Specific Strength Training

Advanced fitness conditioning for climbing is all about the pull muscles. You might take it one step farther and say it's mostly about finger strength. To meet this need, numerous exercises and protocols have been publicized over the years.

David Blocher on Apollo Reed
(5.13a), Summersville Lake, West
Virginia. PHOTO: STEWART GREEN

Everything from fingertip pulls to fingerboards to massive bouldering to various squeeze devices has been used, with mixed results. Ultimately, the usefulness of these exercises depends on a number of things, including their ability to bring about rapid muscular failure and their specificity to finger use while climbing. Let's try to sort things out.

The most specific type of finger training is obviously climbing itself. I strongly advise every serious climber to join a commercial gym or build a home wall. Although indoor walls are generally a poor representation of Mother Nature's rock walls, they are most efficient at providing a sport-specific pump.

Home gyms are key! Just you and some friends climbing, with none of the hassles or waiting common to commercial gyms. And it's always open. For starters, build a 100-square-foot, 50-degree (past vertical) overhanging wall. If space and money are available, add a slightly overhanging traverse wall and some roof climbing. Beyond that, you might add a few panels at 30 and 65 degrees past vertical. Do this and you'll need a commercial gym only for occasional redpoint practice and training endurance.

Before we move on to the details of the advanced program, I must emphasize the context. High-dose strength training is appropriate only for experienced climbers who possess highly developed technical skills. Indoor wall training can elicit a great muscular response, but it does little for training the wide range of techniques needed to excel on real rock. Thus you shouldn't be surprised if, after an extended stretch of indoor training, your return outdoors initially feels a bit off. Rest assured that your technical skills will quickly resurface (assuming you once owned them) and you'll soon be climbing better than ever, thanks to your newfound strength.

The 4-3-2-1 Training Cycle

The practice of cyclic strength training has been around for decades. Applied to climbing, there are several approaches. A number of twelve- to twenty-week training cycles have been published in the climbing magazines over the years, but I feel it's more advantageous to follow a shorter training cycle. Following is a ten-week cycle I developed, called the 4-3-2-1 Cycle. This shorter cycle is mentally easier and may be more effective since you can train maximally on each workout day. (Longer training cycles typically require alternation of easy and hard days to prevent overtraining.)

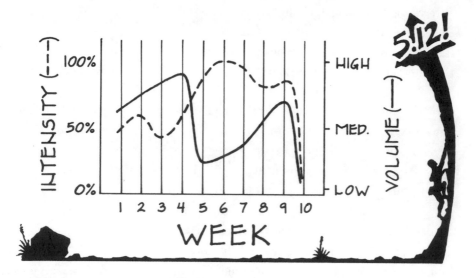

Intensity and volume of climbing and training during the ten-week 4-3-2-1 Cycle.

Any training cycle of reasonable length will be somewhat effective as long as it possesses these four phases: endurance/stamina, maximal strength and power, anaerobic endurance (aka power endurance), and rest. In the ten-week cycle, the lengths of these phases are four weeks, three weeks, two weeks, and one week, respectively. Each is detailed below.

Phase 1—Four Weeks of Forearm Endurance Training

The 4-3-2-1 Cycle begins with the endurance base phase (weeks one through four). The focus here is on climbing—lots of it! During the on season, schedule regular weekend trips and log some redpoints. The off season may be spent mostly in your local climbing gym or on your home wall. Overall volume of climbing should crescendo toward week four, but workout intensity must remain in the midrange at 40 to 80 percent. An occasional maximal-intensity day (as in working a redpoint) won't hurt once a week as part of the high-volume scheme, but the primary goal is to climb many routes a grade or two below your limit. Thus if 5.11 is your limit, strive to crank out many 5.10s.

The endurance phase is the ideal time to work on new technical skills. Do this early in your training sessions or break your climbing day into two parts—a morning skill-training workout and afternoon endurance session. Avoid steep, power-oriented routes as well as anything at your limit. You must not get sucked into high-volume, high-intensity training (phase 3) during these weeks. That'll break the cycle and lower or negate its effectiveness.

Instead overdose on long routes or traverses that are challenging but not quite maximal. Aim for sixty to ninety minutes of nearly continuous climbing with the goal of avoiding a muscle-failing pump! This could be three twenty- to thirty-minute sets on your home wall with a ten-minute break, or twelve six-minute gym routes with a just a few minutes of transition time between climbs. Whatever your approach, incorporate roughly a three-to-one ratio of climbing to rest time.

During the four-week first phase of the training cycle, log a lot of time at the crags. Climb for mileage and tick some redpoints. Here Chris Pegelo sends Chainsaw Massacre (5.12a), Red River Gorge, Kentucky. PHOTO: MIKE LANDKROON

Maximal finger strength is the most valuable commodity for high-end climbers. Assuming your head and technique are together, sending hard routes often comes down to your ability to stick small edges, pull shallow pockets, or hang on to slopers. As Tony Yaniro points out, "If you cannot pull a single hard move, you have nothing to endure." Thus strength training rules over endurance, as declared in Absolute 6.

There has been much debate about the best method to train maximal finger strength. Bouldering has always been held high as a developer of finger strength. Fingerboards became popular in the late 1980s, with campus training and system walls becoming somewhat vogue in the 1990s. Although each of these methods is somewhat effective given the right program, they all fall short of being the best at developing maximal finger strength.

Efficacy of a finger-strengthening exercise is dependent on four fundamental requisites. The more that these requisites are met, the more dramatic the results. Here's a quick look at each:

1. The exercise must be high intensity throughout the entire set. Intensity directly relates to the number of muscular motor units recruited and neurological activity. An exercise performed at near 100 percent intensity throughout the set is the goal.

In climbing, higher intensity is created by increasing wall angle, decreasing hold size, and increasing speed of movement. As you get stronger, however, there's a definite limit to how far you can go with each of these variables—wall angles much past 45 degrees are too rooflike, very small holds are painful to train on, and climbing too fast fosters poor technique. When taken to extremes, all these adjustments will limit your ability to train maximal grip strength.

A better method to up intensity is adding weight to your body. Any power lifter will tell you higher resistance equals higher intensity. Adding just 10 to 15 pounds causes a huge increase in intensity on overhanging walls and will yield a leap in finger strength in just a few weeks. Interestingly, very few climbers are aware of this fact.

2. The exercise must produce rapid *muscular* failure, not failure due to technique. It's universally accepted that strength training must produce muscular failure during the anaerobic phase of exercise. In the weight-lifting world, muscular failure in five to ten reps is considered ideal. This is also valid for our sport but translates to high-intensity climbing that produces failure in ten to twenty total hand movements. In climbing, however, there's always the lingering question of whether failure resulted from maxed-out muscles or not being able to do a move. Thus the best exercise for training grip strength would reduce the technical requirements as much as possible and eliminate training of footwork or arm positions (as in System Training).

3. The exercise must be specific to climbing positions and movements. Strength gains resulting from a certain exercise are specific to situations involving similar position and movement. The greater the difference between the exercise and sport use, the less the strength will transfer. Thus the best strength-training exercise for climbing would involve actual climbing movements, whereas an exercise performed while standing or hanging would transfer less.

4. The exercise must focus on a specific grip position for an entire set. In climbing, the rock dictates a random use of many different grip positions. Since strength is specific to each grip position, such cycling of grips allows you to climb much longer than if you use the same grip repeatedly. That's great if you are climbing for performance—but for the purpose of training grip strength, it stinks! That's why a full season of climbing will build endurance but leave you with the same maximal finger strength as the previous year.

Effective finger-strength training must hammer a specific grip until failure. Due to the limited transfer of strength from one grip to another, you'll need to train all the basic grip positions, including crimp, half crimp, pinch, and the three two-finger pocket combinations or "teams." Isolate and strengthen these grips, and there will be enough near transfer to cover just about any novel grip position you encounter on the rock.

Finger Training Methods—How Do They Stack Up?

	#1—High Intensity?	#2—Rapid Failure?	#3—Specific Movement?	#4—Isolate Grips?
Bouldering	yes	maybe	yes	no
Fingerboard	yes	yes	no	yes
Campus training	yes	yes	no	some
Hypergravity Isolation Training (HIT)	yes	yes	yes	yes

Let's analyze three popular methods for strengthening the fingers plus a new exercise and protocol I've developed. How well each exercise method meets the fundamental requisites (discussed above) will determine its effectiveness.

BOULDERING: The common belief that bouldering is the best finger-strength exercise is wrong for two reasons. First, failure may result from inability to do a move before you reach absolute muscular failure. Furthermore, bouldering inevitably involves a variety of grip positions. This cycling of grips is great for training anaerobic endurance but misses the mark for building maximal strength.

FINGERBOARD: Proper fingerboard training will develop some strength gains. A one-minute set of brief, repetitive, high-intensity hangs (add weight) on a single

Mike McGill throwing a powerful bouldering move at Fontainbleau, France.

grip position meets three of the four requirements. Specificity to climbing movement is not satisfied, however, due to the straight arms and dangling legs. This downfall limits transfer to the rock. Still, it's better than no finger training at all.

CAMPUS TRAINING: Popularized in the 1990s, campus training involves no-feet, high-intensity lunging between simple holds on an overhanging wall. This strenuous exercise maximally stimulates the neuromuscular system and thus develops upper-body power and maximal contact strength—that's good. Like fingerboard training, however, campusing lacks specificity to body use on rock in most situations—that's not good. What's more, campus training naturally focuses on the open-hand grip while neglecting others.

Of course, any type of campus training requires a significant base strength to get started—if you don't have a pretty savage grip already, it may feel impossible. Finally, the dynamic, high-stress nature of campus training makes it a very dangerous exercise for nonelite climbers, and it should not be used by anyone with a history of finger tendon injuries.

HYPERGRAVITY ISOLATION TRAINING (aka Hörst Isolation Training): Advanced climbers have experimented with weighted climbing for years—the results have been mixed and enthusiasm so-so. Hypergravity Isolation Training (HIT) is a highly refined and extremely effective method of weighted climbing I developed in the mid-1990s. HIT workouts meet all four of the above requisites and produce almost immediate, quite noticeable gains in maximal finger strength! HIT involves high-intensity (adding weight to your body simulates what you might call "hypergravity") climbing on identical HIT Strips mounted on a 50-degree overhanging wall.

Even more exciting is that HIT workouts (unlike campus training) can be performed by all but beginner and severely out-of-shape climbers. Still, you must proceed carefully. This training method simulates hypergravity—greater than gravity's normal resistance to climbing—and thus is more stressful than normal climbing. HIT workouts are but part of a great overall training program and are best performed only during phase 2 of the ten-week training cycle. For information on building an HIT wall and performing the HIT workout, see Appendix A.

Phase 3—Two Weeks of Anaerobic-Endurance (A-E) Training

Assuming you have enough strength to do the individual moves on a route, it's your anaerobic endurance (aka power endurance, though this is a scientifically incorrect term) that's put to the test. Continuous difficult bouldering or climbing—with only brief shakeouts—that produces muscular failure in approximately three to five minutes is the preferred method. Vary the intensity of the climbing back and forth between 60 and 95 percent over the three- to five-minute burn. This is much like interval training used by runners—the gold standard for developing anaerobic endurance. You can perform an effective A-E workout using the HIT Strip system or on a steep home wall. See Appendix A for details.

Interestingly, many climbers already train this way on indoor bouldering caves and at their home crags. Why then don't they all become superstrong and end up sending 5.12s in their sleep?

PHASE	WEEK OF CYCLE	DAY OF WEEK						
		1	2	3	4	5	6	7
ENDURANCE	1		•		•		•	•
	2			•	•		•	
	3		•	•	•	•		•
	4		•	•		•	•	•
MAXIMUM STRENGTH	5			•			•	
	6			•			•	
	7			•			•	
ANAEROBIC ENDURANCE	8			•			•	
	9	•			•			•
REST	10							

Dots indicate active days—training or climbing—during the ten-week 4-3-2-1 Cycle.

Answer: Anaerobic-endurance training places high levels of stress on the nervous system and muscles. Beyond a certain point the body cannot recover from these workouts. About two weeks seems to be the limit if you climb regularly. Ironically, many climbers train this way for months on end and then wonder why they don't get stronger. Undoubtedly, they are overtraining, and injury, sickness, and long plateaus in performance are the common legacy of such training.

Remember that the effectiveness of the 4-3-2-1 Cycle results largely because each of the active phases targets a different energy pathway. Getting the maximum training response therefore demands that you stick to the program and train exactly as each phase specifies. Break the cycle and you break its efficacy.

Phase 4—One Week of Rest and Recovery

The ten-week cycle concludes with a full week off from training *and* climbing. During the nine preceding weeks, you hit your body relentlessly two to four days per week. Although one to three days of rest between individual workouts is usually enough for muscular recovery, wear and tear on the joints and tendons, central fatigue of the nervous system, and mental fatigue continue to accumulate. This rest week goes a long way toward clearing the slate of central fatigue, as well as giving connective tissues time to catch up in the healing and recovery process.

At the end of your rest week, evaluate your mental and physical state. If you're not feeling 100 percent ready to go, take another three to fourteen days off. An extra week or two invested in healing a finger tendon strain has greater long-term value than the few workouts you'll miss. Any loss of strength or skill during this time off will be slight and will disappear quickly upon resumption of training.

Advanced Fitness Conditioning Tips

- The 4-3-2-1 Training Cycle will produce continuous, noticeable results. On a calendar, plan out successive ten-week training cycles. Use the cycles year-round, breaking only for long road trips or during your annual few weeks off from climbing.

- Continuous bouldering or lapping routes for twenty to thirty minutes at moderate intensity is excellent endurance training. In using the 4-3-2-1 Cycle, keep the four-week phase 1 all about training endurance, not strength. Chalk up lots of medium-intensity climbing and avoid the deep pump. Three to five days of climbing per week is best.

- Effective maximal finger-strength training must be high intensity and specific to climbing movement, isolate specific grips, and produce rapid failure. Hypergravity Isolation Training (HIT) is the ideal exercise for the three-week second phase of the 4-3-2-1 Cycle. Alternatively, wear a 10- to 20-pound weight belt while bouldering on nonpainful holds on an overhanging wall. Use a work-to-rest ratio of roughly one to three.

- Train anaerobic endurance by sending numerous high-intensity boulder problems or short routes with only brief rests in between. In using this interval training approach on roped routes, strive for five to ten maximal burns with only a couple of minutes' rest in between. For a bouldering workout, shoot for ten to twenty problems with only brief rests between problems.

Preventing Injury and Speeding Recovery

Injury prevention and accelerating recovery are two subjects ignored or over-looked by the mass of climbers. In order to maximize your long-term rate of improvement, however, you must act in disciplined ways to mitigate injury and speed recovery between workouts or days of climbing.

Supplemental Training for Muscle Balance

Climbing works the finger flexor muscles to death but does little to strengthen the extensor muscles (on the back of your forearms) and the pronator muscles (which hold your hand stable as you pull down on the rock). Over time you will likely develop muscular imbalances that leave you susceptible to elbow tendinitis—either medial epicondylitis (inside elbow) or lateral epicondylitis (outside elbow).

Reverse wrist curls are a great exercise that will help prevent lateral epi-condylitis—inflammation of the tendon origin of the forearm extensors, more popularly known as tennis elbow. Perform these curls religiously at the end of each workout to strengthen your forearm extensors. Three twenty-repetition sets with a light weight go a long way toward preventing this injury. It may also be beneficial to do one set of relatively light reverse wrist curls as you stretch your forearms during the warm-up phase of your workout.

For the pronators you can do a simple pronation exercise with a lightly weighted 12-inch section of broomstick or pronator tube (see page 60). Commit to performing one set of pronators with each arm as a warm-up before climbing, then do two more sets at the end of your workout. This simple exercise does wonders for preventing medial epicondylitis.

Maintaining some semblance of balance in the larger muscles of your upper body is also important. The pull muscles become monstrously strong from climbing, while the push muscles such as the pectorals, deltoids, and triceps fall behind. Push-ups and dips are two exercises that will compensate in these areas without adding much mass. Two or three sets each, twice per week, is usually enough to keep you in balance. This minimalist approach for push-muscle train-ing is ideal. I do not advise any heavy free-weight bodybuilder training for climbers.

1. **Push-ups or light bench press.** Three sets of standard push-ups, twice a week, is enough. Vary the distance between hands if you like, and always go until failure. If you prefer to use a bench press, that's fine—but keep the weights light and the reps high. It's inadvisable to use more than 50 to 75 percent of your body weight.

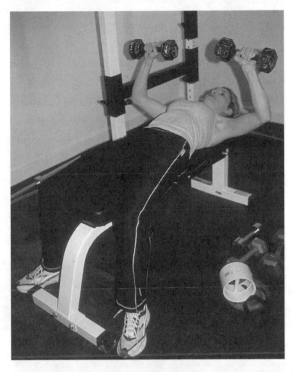

2. **Light shoulder press.** Use dumbbells, a light bar, or a machine and perform three sets of around twenty reps. Total resistance should be limited to between 20 and 40 percent of your body weight. Again, do these just a few days per week.

3. Dips. These are somewhat similar to mantles when performed with your hands in close to your body. Performing three sets to failure, two days per week, will have a positive effect on your climbing. Have a spotter aid you if initially you can't do at least ten reps.

Rest and Recovery from Workouts

As Absolute 8 points out, training does not produce muscular growth or gains in strength. It merely stimulates the body's growth mechanisms into motion. In fact, high-intensity training such as the maximal-strength and anaerobic-endurance phases of the 4-3-2-1 Cycle are catabolic (muscle eating) and fry the nervous system. It's during rest that your body recovers and, with enough rest, rebuilds to a higher level than before.

It's very common for enthusiastic climbers to work out again before completion of the recovery process. Although you may get away with this once in a while (and with less benefit from your workouts), this practice of underresting will eventually lead to a downward spiral of overtraining and, possibly, injury. In my opinion, a good definition of insanity is the continuation of training that produces no obvious, or even negative, results.

Quality rest is a big key to getting stronger, but the exact amount is hard to pin down. There are many factors that contribute to rate of recovery, such as your diet, hours of sleep, rest-day activity, level of fitness, age, and genetics. Another major factor is the intensity level of the workout. Complete recovery from a low-intensity endurance workout may take just twenty-four hours, while a savage four-hour anaerobic endurance workout could require as much as three to five days. Ultimately, you need to be aware of your body's signals and continue with your next workout only when you feel fully recovered.

Nutrition to Speed Recovery

Your muscles can do little rebuilding until you go to sleep, but they can begin restocking glycogen (sugar fuel in the muscle). You can shorten recovery time by starting the glycogen repletion process during cool-down. A sports drink with approximately a four-to-one ratio of carbohydrates to protein is ideal—if you can find one. Otherwise, consume a sugar-based sports drink (like Gatorade) followed by a high-protein drink (such as whey). In the case of a hard workout or full day of climbing, you would want to consume about 100 grams of liquid carbohydrate along with 25 grams of liquid protein. Research has shown that you can accelerate recovery by as much as 50 percent if you drink this combination of carbohydrate and protein within two hours of ending your workout—the sooner, the better.

Next, you want to eat a well-balanced meal comprised of a low-fat protein such as chicken or fish, a liberal serving of vegetables, and a modest portion of pasta. Eat this meal about two hours after your workout to provide an extended "trickle" of nutrients to the body for several more hours. Consider eating additional small "meals" (such as a piece of fruit or balanced-type energy bar) every few hours to keep the trickle going. This is especially important in the twenty-four hours following a hard workout.

Sleep and Grow Strong

The body repairs itself and new growth takes place mainly while you are asleep. Therefore, the amount of sleep you get on the night after a hard workout is as important as your use of proper training exercises and consumption of correct nutrients. Studies of thousands of athletes in many different sports show a dramatic difference in the rate of recovery in those getting nine hours of sleep as opposed to only six. What's more, athletes sleeping nine hours were less likely to get injured or suffer from overtraining.

Granted, if your schedule is anything like mine, there are too few hours in the day already. The good news is the largest sleep requirement is the first night after intense exercise. If at all possible, get eight and a half to nine hours that night. Go to bed earlier as opposed to sleeping in later to log the extra time. Try for seven and a half to eight hours of sleep on the second night, and between six and eight on all successive nights until your next workout. Remember, sleep is an essential part of your training. Don't hesitate to say no to late-night outings or mindless TV watching in favor of getting to bed earlier. In the long run, this practice will make you a stronger and better climber!

Finally, if you work out in the morning or do split workouts, consider a thirty- to sixty-minute nap during the day. This, too, may be hard to pull off, but along with the nutritional regime discussed above, it provides the greatest training and recovery effects.

Injury Prevention and Recovery Tips

- Train your antagonistic muscles frequently to help ward off injury. Consider it mandatory to perform three sets of pronators and three sets of reverse wrist curls as part of every workout (one set during warm-up and two sets at the end of the session). A few sets of push-ups and dips are also advised, twice per week.

- Quality rest is as important as quality stimulus (the workout) for producing gains in strength. It's best not to proceed with your next workout until fully recovered. Use muscle soreness and your overall energy level to gauge where you are in the recovery process. A written record tracking workouts, sleep, diet, and how you feel will improve awareness on this matter.

- Your dietary habits following a workout are key to minimizing recovery time and maximizing muscular restructuring. Consume 50 to 100 grams of simple carbohydrates upon completion of your workout or, better yet, use a four-to-one-ratio (carbohydrate-to-protein) recovery drink. Follow this with a meal containing 20 to 30 grams of protein and a moderate portion of carbohydrate foodstuffs within about two hours.

- At least nine hours of sleep is required for optimal recovery from severe workouts. About eight hours is optimal on other nights.

Mike Freeman on Nectar Vector (5.12d R),
Shawangunks, New York.

PHOTO: MICHAEL MILLER

CHAPTER FOUR

Winning the Head Games

I wanna do something absolutely at my limit, where my whole body is screaming in pain, everything wants to fall off, but I keep on going. —Jerry Moffatt

t's the head games that separate the men (and women) from the boys in this sport. Physical and technical prowess can collapse without a moment's notice if you don't possess a good head. A well-known climbing axiom is that "the greatest ascents result more often from mental breakthroughs than physical." Consider the focus and vision of Wolfgang Güllich sending the steep, one-finger pocketed Action Direct (5.14d) back in 1991; the unwavering motivation and discipline of Lynn Hill to free climb the 3,000-foot Nose of El Capitan in a day; and the laserlike concentration and confidence of John Gill's 1961 solo of the Thimble (5.12b/c or V5)—while wearing hiking boots, no less! Such legendary accomplishments are the result of the synergy of skill, fitness, and mental fortitude. Greatness comes no other way.

In this chapter I touch on eleven elements of the head game. Clearly, all are intertwined, but I've broken them down into more bite-sized chucks and present them in a logical progression. As you read, reflect on your personal head games and consider what improvements can be made. Employ the tip after each section to begin the journey toward some legendary accomplishments of your own!

Motivation Multiplies Talent

Motivation is the foundation for all accomplishments. Natural talent, great genetics, and all the time and money in the world will get you nowhere without motivation. Many great human feats are achieved by modestly talented, even disabled, people who possess heroic levels of motivation. Consider Oprah Winfrey running a full marathon or, more seriously, Hugh Herr climbing a 5.13 just two years after the amputation of his lower legs and blind climber Erik Weihenmayer's daring ascent of Mount Everest. Such brilliant feats are possible only with intense self-motivation.

Consistent, day-to-day motivation to train hard and to push yourself at the crags is a common problem. External stimuli such as aggro tunes or a double espresso merely energize your state at that moment—they do not motivate. Motivation is a twenty-four-hour focus and enthusiasm to do the things that help you toward your goal, while steering clear of anything that might slow the process. Ultimately, it's your expectations and incentives that keep the motivation burning.

Always expect success, whether you're training or climbing. In the gym, expect that the workout will make you stronger and elevate you toward your goals. At the crags, expect you'll send the route—or at least learn a new skill that will make a difference in the future. Believe there's a positive causal connection between the task at hand and your future goals, and motivation will be yours. Conversely, even a fleeting thought that the workout won't help or success is unlikely will hose motivation in an instant.

Incentives to train also enhance motivation. Simple things such as a tick list of to-do routes, a competition you've entered, or a road trip inked in on the calendar will stoke the fires. As the tick-list routes begin to fall or as the competition nears, your motivation will grow stronger still.

Finally, there's the power of visualization to motivate. Whether the task is six months of writing a book about climbing 5.12 or six months training to climb a 5.12, daily visualization of the completed project will power consistent action.

Tip: Unwavering motivation is fundamental to realizing athletic potential. Toward this end, create incentives to train, expect success as you climb, and begin with the end in mind. Motivation will always be yours.

Goals That Compel Action

Most people set goals in the long term—a dream climb, place, event, maybe even grade level of climbing. But to set only long-term goals is to miss the boat to them altogether. In fact, short-term goals are more powerful, because they fuel and steer your boat toward long-term destinations. Start your trek today by establishing some written goals in three time frames: short term (daily), medium term (weekly or monthly), and long term.

Short-term goals are simply a daily to-do list specific to improving your climbing performance. Write them down the night before or as you eat breakfast in the morning. Here are a few examples: If yesterday was a savage maximal-strength workout, your list reads "eat five small carbohydrate and protein meals and get eight and a half hours of sleep." Or if you have a climbing-gym workout scheduled today, set goals specific to training weaknesses, new skills, and a few strength exercises. At the crags, write down the warm-up exercises and routes to do before attempting your redpoint project. No matter what the task, a written list, whether on a Post-it note or in a training log, is the carrot compelling consistent, intelligent actions.

Medium-term planning integrates your training and climbing schedule with the rest of your life. It will optimize your use of time and keep you on the fast track to higher performance. Loosely plan things out on a calendar a few months in advance. First mark in big events such as climbing trips, competitions, work and family obligations, and so forth. Now plot the weekly phases of your training cycle, hopefully fitting them around your big events. In pencil, mark proposed workout, climbing, and rest days, realizing that these days are flexible and can be changed. Finish by jotting down some specific physical and technical gains, as well as a couple of routes you'd like to send in the coming months. Things such as "20 consecutive pull-ups," "improve finger-jamming technique," and "climb the Naked Edge" give additional meaning to the daily grind of training.

When all the important items are in place, the many little, less important things in life can fall in where time allows. I'm talking about the myriad distractions vying for your attention and time—television, parties, surfing the Net, and so forth. Although many of us can be drugged by the instant gratification they offer, medium-term planning will help keep you on track toward more lofty, meaningful accomplishments.

Finally, there are the long-term dream goals floating around in your mind. This might be the grade of climbing to achieve or a specific dream climb. Also, think about where you'd go if time and money weren't an issue. Is there an exotic climbing area you want to travel to? For any chance that these goals will ever become reality, you must liberate them from the dreamland of your mind and put them down in black and white. There's a magical power in writing things down: It makes them believable and therefore achievable.

Tip: Detailed goals compel consistent daily and long-term action. Ask yourself, "What can I do in the next hour, day, week, month, or year to enhance my climbing performance?" Set short-, medium-, and long-term goals accordingly.

Discipline Leads to Excellence

To excel in anything—sport, business, relationships—takes a lot of discipline: discipline to do all the things that point toward your goal and discipline to abstain from the things that move you away from it. When it comes to discipline, there's no high-tech, scientific gobbledygook to talk about; it just comes down to how badly you want it. There are many talented climbers who never became great because they lack discipline—for every two steps forward, they take at least one step back. Conversely, many climbers of average talent have become masters of rock because they cut ties to anything that might hold them back. In the long run their sacrifices paid off by realizing their full potential in this sport.

Certainly, discipline alone does not guarantee success—yet a lack of it goes a long way toward guaranteeing you will fall short of your potential. Examine your discipline by asking yourself these questions.

1. Do I set daily goals that I usually meet?

2. Do I work out and climb only when my body is ready, and take another rest day when I'm still fatigued or sore?

3. Do I most often say no to food and drink that can separate me from my goals, while supplying my body with the fuel and nutrients necessary to train hard and recover quickly?

4. Do I regularly sacrifice late-night TV and social outings so I can get the good night's sleep necessary to fully recover from my training?

5. Do I hang out and climb with positive, motivated people who will help me toward my goals and avoid those with attitudes and habits that will hold me back?

Tip: Discipline is fundamental in the pursuit of excellence. Always distinguish between what's important and what's urgent—they are not the same! Target your attention and time on activities that will bring you closer to your high-value goals, while saying no to many of the popular activities (that consume the masses) that may divert your focus and energy.

Cranking Up Confidence

As much as any other attribute, your level of confidence upon starting a route may predetermine your likelihood of success. Think back to the last time you did a route you had wired. As you prepared for the climb, chances are you felt no

Lauri Stricker advances confidently on Access All Areas (5.11a), Shelf Road, Colorado.

PHOTO: STEWART GREEN

doubt about the results; the route was in the bag. You then, of course, proceeded to send the route in a relaxed, carefree, yet focused state. This experience reflects the dramatic effect that confidence has on performance. But what exactly is confidence, and how is it developed?

Confidence is positive energy, enthusiasm, and high expectancy of success. You climb free, loose, quick, and fluid, and even in the face of pressure remain mentally calm and focused. Such bulletproof confidence does not just appear on the spot by thinking positive thoughts or hoping for the best, however. Confidence is developed beforehand via extensive preparation and experience.

Nothing elicits confidence like having been there before. Thus one of your training goals should be to mimic as best as you can the atmosphere, situations, and terrain of the project or competition for which you're preparing. One great example of this is my friend Mike Freeman's training regimen for the steep, cavernous Hole at the New River Gorge. Noting his discomfort and intimidation the first time he attempted a route out the 30-foot roof, he set out to hang upside down under any object he could find in his hometown in New Jersey. With only marginal indoor walls in his area at the time, he logged some time a few days a week climbing the underside of a playground jungle gym. Although the physical training value of this was minimal, the time spent in the horizontal developed familiarity with the position and thus tremendous confidence. Confidence is a self-fulfilling prophecy, and Mike went on to redpoint a number of hard routes in the Hole that season.

Physical and mental training also build confidence. The strong, dialed-in feeling upon completing a ten-week training cycle makes you more confident on the rock. You can also bolster confidence on the spot by visualizing yourself sending the route or by envisioning past successful climbs of similar type and difficulty. If you sense there's a chink in your armor, adjust or beef up your training program accordingly, as it will serve to crank up your confidence.

Tip: Confidence is essential to peak performance. Always acclimate yourself to the conditions under which you will perform. Use mock events, trial runs, and simulator routes to help build confidence. Transfer emotional resources from the past to the present by vividly visualizing and feeling the emotions of some past successes.

Visualization—Preprogramming the Future

Visualization is a fundamental skill used by top athletes the world over. If you're not actively using visualization, you're missing out on the most powerful smart bomb in a climber's arsenal.

Although similar to the mental rehearsals performed by many climbers, visualization goes beyond the simple task of reviewing sequences. With it you create detailed movies in your head with touch, sound, color, and all the kinesthetic feel of doing a route. These movies aren't just colorful daydreams; they actually help build a mental map to a future, desired reality. Once programmed into the brain, these movies improve your mind–body integration, thereby enhancing your performance on the rock. Your movies become blueprints for action, so make sure they're positive and very detailed. Run and rerun the movies in your mind's eye, and soon they'll become a physical reality!

Visualization can enhance your climbing no matter the situation, whether in competition, on-sight, or working a redpoint. The latter situation is the best for developing the skill. Having already worked a route, you should be able to vividly imagine the feeling of doing the moves, grabbing the holds, milking rests, and so forth. Remember, simply reviewing a sequence in your mind is merely mental rehearsal, not visualization. Elevating your performance with visualization requires that you engage in mental moviemaking complete with all the sensations, sounds, colors, and emotions your imagination can create. The more detailed the visualization, the more the moves will become hardwired into the brain, and the more your subconscious mind will begin to believe in the ascent.

You can also use visualization on routes you've never been on before. The world's best on-sight climbers have mastered the skill of creating a detailed movie of a successful attempt. Some people even create two possible movies of crux sections and then select the one that looks more promising at the time. Study the climb from a few different ground perspectives, noting possible rests, gear placements, and, of course, hidden holds and crux sequences. Next, create a movie of yourself climbing the route—watch from the on-TV, dissociated perspective. Repeat this visualization a few times, then try to reshoot the movie in the associated state where you can live it. The goal is to feel the sensations and experience the situations of actually doing the route.

The above strategy is invaluable for competition climbing. During your preview of the route, gather as much information and shoot as many pictures as possible. In isolation, build your mental movie and run through it in preparation for a flash ascent!

Another popular use of visualization is to "climb" during rest days or while laid up due to injury. Regular visualization of a familiar route or project helps maintain motor skills and route knowledge. A final at-the-crag use is to mentally send your project a few more times when you're physically too burned to climb anymore. The above uses of visualization are certainly more beneficial than doing nothing at all.

Use of the many applications of visualization will dramatically improve your performance in both the short and long term. Always dovetail visualization with actual climbing and training to maintain accuracy of the images, and work to become acutely aware of the feelings and results you get. The more you practice visualization, the sooner you'll master this vital skill.

Tip: Visualization helps preprogram future realities. Use it daily in preparation for training, climbing, or any other important task. Draw all your senses into the images and allow yourself to feel the moves in motion. Make the images as positive and accurate as possible, as visualization can program both good and bad outcomes.

Visualization Tips

- Practice visualization daily. Use the dissociated perspective when reviewing past events, but favor associated visualization when preparing for a future event.

- Incorporate all your senses into your mental movies. Visualization that includes sound, touch, and emotion is most effective.

- Use photographs, beta sheets, and videotape to improve the accuracy of the mental movie.

- Visualize your project route at least once per day. Regular mental practice combined with physical practice is synergistic.

- Edit out negative images from your movie and reshoot the film anytime you gain more information about the climb.

- Use dissociated visualization to prepare for on-sight ascents. This is especially important as part of the risk management process. Use the associated perspective in preparing for a redpoint ascent.

- Establish a regular visualization practice schedule just as you have a regular gym workout schedule. For best results, visualization should be practiced when you are in a deep state of relaxation, such as before falling asleep. Consider using the Progressive Relaxation Sequence described on page 92.

Developing Preclimb Rituals

Rituals are powerful anchors for consistent performance. Rituals are used by all elite athletes. Observe Barry Bonds stepping up to the plate, Tiger Woods preparing for a birdie putt, or Kobe Bryant setting up for a foul shot—their preparation and setup are identical each time. Every tiny detail is programmed into a mental checklist, including posture, breathing, visualization, and final thoughts. For these athletes, habitual rituals produce consistently positive results.

Develop your own rituals based on past experiences. Whether a list of activities or meals and a to-bed time for the day before a competition or a mental checklist of preclimb preparations, consistent rituals yield consistent results. What did you do and think in the minutes leading up to some of your particularly brilliant ascents? What did you do the day before the climb that helped maximize your energy and mental state? Awareness of all the little things is key! The more detailed and lengthy the rituals, the greater the effect. Include everything you can think of, from when and how you lace your shoes, to tying in to the rope, to chalking up and taking a few slow, deep breaths before you start climbing. You may even want to model some elements of rituals performed by other successful climbers.

Precompetition rituals are especially useful as time markers leading up to a competition. The ritual may begin days before the event and count down to the minutes before the climb as you perform your warm-up, stretching, visualization, and preparatory self-talk. As you step up to the wall, your focus will be laserlike and your confidence high, knowing your tried-and-true ritual has placed you in the ideal performance state of past successes.

Tip: Consistent preclimb rituals give birth to consistent performances. Establish a detailed preclimb routine, including all preparatory tasks from gearing up to visualization practice. When the ritual becomes tried and true, stick to it! If you are a competition climber, develop a separate precompetition ritual beginning several days before the competition and continuing down to the moment you get on the wall.

Reasonable Fears Versus Unreasonable Fears

The no-fear mentality is for buffoons, beer-guzzling frat boys, and couch potatoes. In climbing, reasonable fears keep you alive long enough to realize your potential and to send a long lifetime's worth of stellar routes. For example, fear of taking a ground fall compels you to seek good protection on the lead and to drag a rope in the first place.

It's unreasonable fears that derail performance. Things such as fear of falling on a well-protected route, fear of performance pains, fear of failure, and fear of embarrassment must all be nixed. There are also preclimb fears such as "I might be too tall," "too short," or "too weak" to do the climb—left unchecked, these fears give birth to reality. Finally, there are subconscious, preprogrammed fears that are the root of many of the dumb things that seem to just happen. Have you ever fallen after the crux when the route is in the bag? Or have you slipped off a large hold or botched a wired sequence even though you felt in control? It may be that such mistakes are the result of unchallenged inner fears, not lack of ability.

Deal with your fears head-on. Start by writing down recurrent fears that regularly hurt your performance. If you can't think of any on the spot, go for a climb and pay special attention to every preclimb thought and while-you-climb concern. As the fears reveal themselves, use logic and reason to specifically counter each. This is usually pretty easy, but if no logical counter is evident, the fear may be reasonable.

Dealing with fear is an ongoing process—our fears are always changing. Review each poor performance and identify which fear(s) may have contributed to your difficulties. To help you with this analysis, here's a primer on four basic climbing fears: fear of falling, fear of pain, fear of failure, and fear of embarrassment.

Fear of Falling

Fear of falling is inherent to climbing. Interestingly enough, it's not really falling that we fear, but not knowing what the fall will be like. This explains why your first fall on a route is the scariest, while subsequent falls are often much less stressful. Beginners probably need some hands-on proof that falls can be safe. The best way for a would-be leader to gain trust in the system is by taking some intentional falls. Find a steep climb with good protection, use a good rope (and double-check your knot and buckle), and take some falls.

Start off with 2-footers and build up to 15-footers. A more experienced climber fearful of falling on an upcoming on-sight climb can counter the fear during the preclimb warm-up. The tactic here is to mentally replay some past inconsequential falls and remind yourself that falls on this climb will be no different (if that is indeed the case—some falls are obviously deadly, and only a fool would ignore that possibility).

Fear of Pain

When pushing your limits, fear of pain and discomfort can become a critical weakness. This fear causes you to give up long before your body has reached its

Multipitch climbing in the mountains can be as testing mentally as it is physically. Here two climbers push up The Flame (5.10), Pikes Peak, Colorado.

PHOTO: STEWART GREEN

physical limitations. The pain of climbing a continuously strenuous route is akin to that of running a mile at full speed—it freaking hurts! Fortunately, the pain is brief and the challenge pays big dividends. Decide to push yourself a bit farther into the discomfort zone each time you're on a hard route. Soon your pain threshold will be redefined, as will your limits on the rock!

Fear of Failure

This deep-seated fear is instilled during childhood when almost every action is classified by our family, teachers, and friends as either a success or a failure. We've all had childhood situations where the fear of failure was so gripping we became immobilized and time seemed to stop. Fortunately, adults generally don't react quite that intensely, but it is still common for us to imagine all the bad things that could possibly go wrong. Once triggered, these negative thoughts can snowball and, more often than not, become self-fulfilling prophecies.

In climbing, fear of failure causes you to hold back. Your attack on a route becomes less aggressive than required, you'll find yourself second-guessing sequences in the midst of doing them, your breathing will become shallow, and your grip will tighten. You may even fall prey to paralysis by analysis.

Eliminate fear of failure one of two ways. First, focus on what is probable instead of what is possible. Sure, it's human nature to always consider the worst-case scenario, but it almost never comes true. Counter these thoughts by considering what is probable and realistic based on past experiences. The second method to nix this fear is to focus all your attention on the process of climbing and forget about the possible outcomes. Concentrate on the things immediate to your performance like precise foot placements, relaxing your grip, moving quickly onto the next rest position, and so forth. Your limited supply of energy is too valuable to waste worrying about how high you will climb or the eventual results. Let that take care of itself.

Remember that in sports there are no failures, only results. If you fall off the first move of a route, it is a result of not paying attention to the move, not because you are a worthless individual. The results might not be ideal, but they do contain hints for improvement. Take these clues and resolve to persevere despite setbacks; you will grow to become an uncommonly successful climber.

Fear of Embarrassment

Finally, there is fear of embarrassment. Get over this now, or you'll never fully enjoy this sport or reach your potential. Occasional bad performance days are inevitable. Instead of trying to avoid them, simply accept that they happen, analyze why they happened, then bury them. With this attitude you will be free to try chancy moves and risk an occasional mistake. In the long run risking mistakes will pay off with the reward of some brilliant ascents. Surely this is better than embracing the critics and accepting mediocrity all the time.

Don't forget that your friends know how good a climber you are, and they won't think any worse of you because of a poor performance. Anyone else critical of you really doesn't matter. Work on improving your self-confidence and don't let the criticisms of others invade your thoughts. Engage the route, disengage from thoughts of anything else, and just send it!

Tip: Determine whether your fears are reasonable or unreasonable. Heed the reasonable fears, but challenge and laugh in the face of your unreasonable fears. Relaxation and reason are an effective antidote to most unfounded fears encountered on the rock. Focus on what is probable and not on the remote worst-case outcome.

Turning Down the Pressure

Pressure is not inherently good or bad. It's your ability to control and react to pressure that determines its value. You've probably experienced high-pressure situations where nervousness, anxiety, tightness, and lack of focus prevailed, ultimately dooming your performance. Times like these make you dream of no-pressure situations—surely that would be the ideal. Right?

Well, actually not. Some degree of pressure is good. It energizes you and enhances your focus on the task at hand. Remember the pressure of cramming the night before a big exam? Moderate pressure acts as a bit of a "stick," and when combined with a tasty "carrot" (the goal), the results can be stellar. Learning to use this good pressure and eliminate the bad pressure is key.

The control knob to pressure is completely in your hands! Realize that while you will never have control over all elements of a situation, you do have control over your reactions to them. Psychologists explain that no one makes you feel pressure, fear, anger, or frustration but you. Either you allow yourself to feel that way, or you empower someone else to make you feel that way. Acknowledge that you are at the helm of your emotions. Work for constant awareness of how you feel and why. Only then can you make the necessary changes to foster optimal performance.

Let's consider a few ways to optimize pressure in stressful climbing situations, whether at the crag preparing for a redpoint or in isolation at a competition. The goal is to maintain the positive pressures while eliminating the negative.

Positive pressure evolves from effective preparations leading up to the event.

For instance, a good training program, sound nutrition, proper rest, and a good support team will leave you anticipating a solid, successful performance. You'll be focused and optimistic, ready to get to the climb and shred. Such positive pressure is the antithesis of the dread, anxiety, and negative attitude that can result from poor preparations such as training too little (or, more likely, over-training), too little sleep, and poor nutrition.

Assuming you make it to the event positive and upbeat, your next goal is to maintain this state and ward off all the negative pressures trying to infect you. A solid and very detailed preclimb ritual goes a long way toward this end. Still, some negative tension or anxiety is often impossible to avoid. Use relaxation (see the Progressive Relaxation Sequence below) to deflate such negative pressure and maintain your ideal performance state.

Tip: Moderate pressure—not the absence of pressure—produces top performances. Learn to foster good pressure and nix bad pressure; remember, you are in the driver's seat. Your actions and thoughts in the days and hours leading up to the event determine your pressure levels. Use relaxation as your on-the-spot antidote to negative pressures that try to invade.

Progressive Relaxation Sequence

Perform the following procedure at least once a day. I find it most useful during a midday break, as part of a long rest period at the crag, or last thing before falling asleep. Initially, the process will take about fifteen minutes. With practice you'll be able to move quickly through the sequence and reach a state of complete relaxation in less than five minutes. Concentrate on only flexing the muscle(s) specified in each step. This is an invaluable skill you will find very handy when using the ANSWER Sequence discussed later.

1. Go to a quiet location and sit or lie in a comfortable position.

2. Close your eyes and begin by taking five deep belly breaths. Inhale slowly through your nose to a slow, silent count of five, then gradually exhale through your mouth to a slow, silent ten-count.

3. Keeping your eyes closed and maintaining slow, relaxed breathing, tense the muscles in your right lower leg for five seconds. Feel the tension in your right foot and calf muscles, then let go and relax the muscles completely. Compare the difference in sensation between the tense and the relaxed state. Repeat this process with the left lower leg. Now, with both lower-leg areas relaxed, say to yourself, "My feet and lower legs feel warm and light." Upon saying this a few times, the muscles in this area will drop into a deep state of relaxation.

4. Next, perform the same sequence in the muscles of the upper leg (one leg at a time). Tense the muscles in your upper leg for five seconds, then relax them. After doing this with both legs, finish up by thinking, "My upper legs feel warm and light." Feel all tension dissolve as your upper legs drop into deep relaxation.

5. ow repeat this process in your hands and lower arms. Begin by tensing the muscles below your right elbow by making a tight fist for five seconds; then relax these muscles completely. Repeat this with the left hand and forearm, and conclude with the mantra, "My hand and forearm muscles feel warm and light."

6. Repeat this procedure on the muscles in the upper arm.

7. Next, shift the focus to the many muscles of the torso (chest, abdomen, back, and shoulder area). Repeat the process exactly.

8. Conclude with the muscles of the face and neck.

9. You should now be in a deep state of relaxation (possibly, you will have fallen asleep by now). Mentally scan from head to toe for any isolated pockets of remaining tension, and drain them with the "warm and light" mantra.

10. At this point you can open your eyes and return to work or climbing with a renewed sense of calm and focus. Or you can leverage this relaxed state by performing some mind programming—that is, visualization of the process of reaching some goal or the act of climbing some project route.

Focus—The Mind's Hold on the Rock

The ability to narrow and maintain focus is an invaluable mental skill. Widely used, but often misunderstood in the context of a climber's lexicon, the word *focus* refers to a laserlike concentration of mental energy placed on the most important task at any given instant. Since in climbing, every movement possesses a different most important task, you must learn to direct and redirect pinpoint focus on the specific finger or foot placement most critical at each instant.

Think about focus as a narrowing of your concentration. Much like a zoom lens on a camera, you must zoom in and magnify a specific, critical task—toeing

Eric McCallister staying focused as he on-sights Strawberry Jam Direct (5.10c), Rocks State Park, Maryland.

in on a small pocket, placing and pulling on a manky finger jam, or shifting your weight to just the right balance point. Without this tight focus, your foot may pop or your hand may slip or overgrip, and your chance of failure increases.

The most difficult part of focus is learning to zoom in and out quickly from a pinpoint focus to a more wide-angle perspective. The wide-angle mode is used when scoping a sequence ahead and planning a strategy. When climbing, zoom in tightly as you high-step on a dime edge, lock off a hold, or float a deadpoint. The key is learning to switch your point of focus rapidly—much like a laser light show—from one critical task to the next. All the while you ward off outside distractions that threaten to grab and divert your focus away from the rock— certainly not the easiest job in the world. The good news is that there's a prescription to improve your focus. No, not Ritalin, but a simple focus-training exercise you can use at the gym or crag.

Train focus on a route you know that's about one full grade below your on-sight ability. Climb the whole route (ideally on toprope) while trying to maintain focus on a single aspect of movement. For instance, focus only on hand placements. As you climb, find the best way to grab each hold, use the minimum amount of grip strength to stick it, and feel how your purchase changes as you pull on the hold (for example, can you relax your grip more with changing body position or must it tighten?). Place as little focus as is safely possible in other areas such as your feet, balance, belayer, and so forth. For now these areas must take care of themselves; let your sixth sense handle the job.

This exercise is indeed difficult. Your thoughts will wander, and distractions from the ground will occasionally grab your attention. When this occurs, simply redirect your focus to the predetermined task and continue on. Part of the benefit of this exercise is sharpened awareness of when focus is lost and the ability to return it to the desired task. Repeat this drill regularly but with different focus (feet, weight shifts, relaxed movement, and so forth) each time. Work to increase the length of time you can maintain a singular focus. This builds mental endurance. Eventually, you can modify the exercise by switching your focus quickly and without interruption among the various critical tasks involved in climbing a complete route.

Tip: Focus enhances the mind–body–rock connection and, thus, the odds of success. Commit a few weeks to actively training focus. After approximately ten focus-training sessions, you'll begin to feel more connected to the rock and more focused in the midst of stressful situations. Your performance will soar.

Maintaining Control and Poise

Emotional control in sports, also called poise, is fundamental to optimal performance. Dealing with pressure before you climb (as discussed earlier) is a good start, but controlling emotion as you climb is just as important and often much more difficult. Ultimately, you must be able to rein in your emotions and react constructively to any errors or surprises as you climb; otherwise you'll forever be stuck climbing way below your true potential. It's natural for nervous energy and emotions to rise as you perform in a sport such as climbing—it happens to the very best. It's how you deal with it and how often you deal with it that makes the difference.

One effective approach is to break the climb into many small parts, each ending at a decent rest position. Memorize the exact rest locations and, if possible, the body position to be used at each of these break points. (This is something you should add into your preclimb visualization ritual.) At these predetermined spots you will zero your emotions and tensions and gather yourself for the next part of the climb. An effective method for doing this is the ANSWER Sequence (see page 98 for details).

ANSWER is a simple, effective means of maintaining complete control of your mind and body in the midst of a difficult climb. In centering, you deliberately direct your thoughts inward (and away from the climb for a moment) to check and adjust your breathing and level of muscular tensions and to counter any self-defeating thoughts. Scan your body for undesirable changes that have taken place since the last break point—for instance, rapid breathing, overgripping holds, and tightening of antagonistic muscles. Make immediate corrections before the problem snowballs. Otherwise, you will become a climber out of control with an early and ugly end to your climbing guaranteed. Worse yet, no one will want to climb with you if you're spastic and spewing curses.

Practice ANSWER at home, at the gym, or while climbing known routes. As with any skill, you need to practice regularly to become proficient in its use. Do so and in just a few weeks you'll be able to center yourself on any climb, anywhere, and in just a few seconds.

Tip: Controlling emotions as you climb is tantamount to controlling your performance outcome. Break every climb into logical parts defined by rest positions. At these break points, perform the ANSWER Sequence to reset your emotions and renew your optimal performance state for next part of the climb.

Poise is at a premium when a route changes character on you. Here the author moves from the security of a crack up onto the delicate micro edges on the upper portion of Misfits (5.11b/c), Joshua Tree, California.

PHOTO: R. KYLE HÖRST

Perform the ANSWER Sequence before and during each climb and in everyday situations where you need to control tension, anxiety, and focus. Initially, this six-step procedure will take a few minutes to perform. With practice you'll be able to go through it in about ten seconds—perfect for use at marginal rest positions where getting centered could make the difference between success and failure.

Step 1. Awareness* of rising tension, anxiety, or negative thoughts.

Acute awareness of unfavorable mental and physical changes is fundamental to optimal performance. It takes a conscious effort to turn your thoughts away from the outer world toward your inner world. Peak performers habitually make these tension checks every few minutes, so they can nix any negative changes before they snowball out of control. Make this your goal.

Step 2. Normalize* breathing.

In climbing, your breathing should be as relaxed (basically involuntary or unconscious) and regular as it would be while on a fast walk. Unfortunately, many climbers hold their breath while in the midst of a crux sequence, then breathe heavily afterward in order to catch their breath. This process creates tension and degrades performance. Your goal is smooth, even, normal breathing throughout the climb.

Step 3. Scan* for specific areas of muscular tension.

In this step you perform a tension check. Scan all your muscles in a quick sweep to locate pockets of tightness. Commonly tight areas are the forearms (are you overgripping?), shoulders, upper back, chest, abdominals, and calves. The best way to relax a specific muscle is to consciously contract that muscle for a few seconds, then relax it and visualize the tension draining from it like air from a balloon (this is also known as the Differential Relaxation Sequence).

Step 4. Wave *of relaxation.*

Upon completing the tension check above, take a single deep breath and feel a wave of relaxation wash from your head to your toes.

Step 5. Erase *thoughts of past events (or the possible future) and focus on the present.*

This step involves freeing your mind from the ball and chain of undesirable past events. There is no benefit to pondering the last failed attempt or the blown sequence you just barely fought through. Let go of the past and do not ponder the future—thoughts of the past and future are enemies of excellence in the present. Refocus on and engage the present moment.

Step 6. Reset *posture and flash a smile.*

It is amazing how much positive energy you can generate simply by resetting your posture and flashing a smile. This final step of the ANSWER Sequence will leave you in a peak performance state and ready to climb into the zone. Trust your skills, have fun, and let the outcome take care of itself.

Self-Talk Yourself to Success

Much of this chapter has been about increasing awareness of mind and body. Neither can be ignored—they are inseparable and intimately affect each other. A simple example of this is that preclimb shakes can make you anxious, and anxiety can give you preclimb shakes. To combat this inside-out or outside-in self-destruction, you've been presented with several effective tools such as ANSWER, visualization, preclimb rituals, and focus training. This chapter concludes with one more powerful self-management tool: self-talk.

Whether you are aware of it or not, this is something you undoubtedly do already to some degree. *Conscious* use of self-talk is the goal, however, and it's paramount to maximizing performance.

We think in pictures and words. The pictures we see and the words we say are the seeds of reality. Earlier I discussed the importance of controlling the mental images and making movies via visualization. This last section is about tuning into the constant chatter of words in your head and using it to affect reality as well. This is your self-talk.

Self-talk can affect sport success as much as training habits and technical skills. As an example, let's consider two climbers of equal fitness and skills, but vastly different self-talk. Before attempting the same climb, they each think to themselves:

CLIMBER A	CLIMBER B
"This route looks harsh."	"This route looks challenging."
"I hope I don't fall."	"I'll give it my best effort."
"I might be too short."	"A slight physique is my advantage."
"It feels too hot to climb my best."	"My muscles feel warm and energized."
"Many people are watching me."	"Focus on the process, not outcome."
"I feel nervous."	"I'm confident, centered, and ready."
"It might be too pumpy for me."	"I've trained hard, it looks doable."

Which climber do you think will have the better performance? Climber A is indulging in self-limiting thoughts that almost certainly are the seeds for his upcoming failure. Meanwhile Climber B is affirming her preparedness and considering the upside to the weather and her physique. Your goal is to emulate the positive approach of Climber B and ward off the negative psyche of Climber A. Let's look at both.

Negative self-talk is insidious because you may have been saying such things for so long that you're unaware of it or even think it's normal. Thus becoming aware of all your self-talk at home, school, work, and while climbing is the first step. You must break down the negatives and rebuild them into valid positives. Be aware that simply drowning yourself in false positives holds no value. If you're short, for instance, telling yourself "I'm tall" is a farce. Instead, counter with a valid reason why being short and light might be an advantage on the climb.

Effective self-talk is affirmation of your preparedness and positive attributes, not hopes or wishes of what you want to happen. Like Climber B, your self-talk should relate to positives in the reality of the given situation. Affirm why you should do well and believe it wholeheartedly.

Many top athletes actively use self-talk as they perform to enhance focus, remind themselves of fundamental skills, and counter false negative thoughts. When climbing, you might say to yourself, "Relax grip," "Focus on the feet," "Keep breathing," "Good rest ahead—hang in there," "Get centered," "Only one more hard move," "Use straight-arm hangs," "Climb faster," and so forth. But keep the affirmations (valid positives) going long after the climb is over, whether at home, work, the gym, or wherever. Like your muscles, your mental state is constantly in flux—you're either building it up or tearing it down. And always base your self-talk on what you have, not on what you don't have. In the long term its influence on your climbing (and life) will be remarkable!

Tip: Positive self-talk enhances your overall mental state and the odds of success. Use self-talk to counter false negatives, remember skills, and reinforce your positive qualities. Make your self-talk intensely action-oriented and empowering. Use positive self-talk throughout the day and in all aspects of your life—you cannot just turn it on when you go climbing.

Lisa Ann Hörst on her second 5.12 redpoint, Lovelife (5.12b), Lancaster, Pennsylvania.

Climbing Your First 5.12 (and Beyond!)

The best way to push yourself the hardest and do the most amazing things is by having fun—not going up on something because someone said it would be impressive, but because you can't imagine any other place on the planet you'd rather be.
—Peter Croft

Training on a home wall or at a climbing gym can be a blast, but nothing beats finding a beautiful route at some crag and on-sighting it—well, maybe falling in love with a rad-looking project, working it, training for it, dreaming of it, and then sending it does . . . In any case, when reading a performance guidebook such as this one, it's easy to forget what this sport is all about—getting outside and climbing rock!

For many readers the goal is to climb 5.12, while for others it may be 5.8 or 5.14. The numbers really don't matter; it's pushing your boundaries that counts. This gives you that "must-experience-it-to-understand-it" climber's high, and it builds character and confidence that carry over into all other aspects of your life.

In this chapter I'll touch on some of the basics relating to your performance at the crags, from picking a route to tricks for tough climbs. The meat of this chapter is strategic and tactical information for on-sighting routes and working redpoint projects. I do not cover issues of safety or belaying or the hundreds of specific movements and body-positioning skills. Consult other books in the How to Climb series for specific instruction in these areas.

Consider that performing near your physical limit, whether on-sight or redpoint, is very mental. Although I will discuss some tactical head games in this chapter, see chapter 4 for a comprehensive look into mental training.

Selecting the Right Route

Proper route selection plays a vital role in determining the learning value and success-building potential of a day at the crags. Following are three issues to consider in choosing the perfect line.

Practice or Performance?

Choose a route according to the day's goal—climbing for *practice* or *performance*. If skill practice is the goal, pick a route that works one of your known weaknesses. For instance, if you are intimidated or have technical difficulty on roof routes, select a route (upon completing a few warm-up climbs) that features a challenging roof or tiered overhang. Whatever your weakness—be it slabs, thin fingercracks, steep routes, or thin vert faces—it's your commitment to work this frequently that will make you better.

If performance is the goal du jour, by all means exploit your strengths! Pick an inspiring-looking route that focuses on what you do well. What type of climb do you find most exciting and enjoyable? Knowing this will help you find the perfect route to exploit your strengths and climb your very best. Of course, exploiting your strengths won't make you better, but it will make for some brilliant ascents—the goal of performance days.

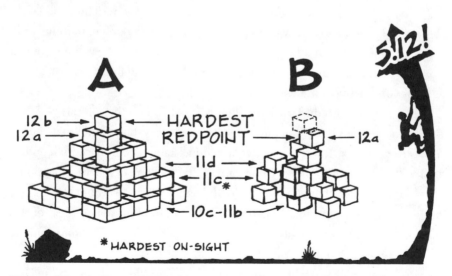

Climber A has built a solid foundation for progressing into 5.12 with many ascents near her on-sight level. Climber B has not consolidated his current on-sight level and will struggle to advance.

On-Sight or Redpoint?

Your next decision is whether you'll climb on-sight or work a route for redpoint. If you've found a climb you like, the grade may determine this matter for you. It's unlikely you'll on-sight more than a letter above your hardest on-sight to date (although it can happen).

If you have a wide choice of suitable routes at your grade, favor on-sight over redpoint at a two-to-one ratio. Both are valuable experiences, but on-sight climbing provides greater potential for learning. Overemphasis on redpointing is an all-too-common mistake of climbers in search of big numbers. They spend a lot of the time flailing on the rock, learn very little, and only occasionally succeed on such difficult routes. Exclusive use of this approach can demoralize and injure you, and has less learning and practice value than on-sighting slightly easier routes.

Consolidate Your Grade-Level Ability

Two common mistakes in cragging are working redpoint routes too hard for you and on-sighting routes too far below your limit. It's better to focus your climbing near your maximal ability level. Such consolidation of ability at a grade level establishes the foundation from which you can push the envelope just a bit farther.

Except for warm-up climbs, pick routes within one number grade of your hardest on-sight. For instance, if 5.11c is your top on-sight level, select routes between 5.10c and 5.11d to on-sight. Sending several routes at this grade solidifies your ability, while hiking a zillion 5.10a's or hoping to "get lucky" on a 5.13a holds little value.

As for picking a grade to redpoint, work routes between 5.11d and 5.12c, as per the example above. Routes in the low end of this range may go in just two or three tries, while the hard lines may take several days. Avoid getting involved in projects more than a number grade beyond your best on-sight (no routes beyond 5.12c in this example). You'll use up too much time on too many climbing days when you could be consolidating your current ability level. The sooner you firm up skill and confidence at your current level, the faster you'll progress for real beyond it!

Use the four climbing-grade pyramids located appendix B, in the back of this book, to plot your progress toward 5.12. Fill in the route name and date of each redpoint. Try to complete one row of blocks at a time. If you find just the right route, however, don't hesitate to push on to the next level.

Tips for Picking the Right Route

- Determine if the day is for practice or performance. On practice days choose route types with which you have difficulties. Conversely, use performance days to exploit your strengths for great performances.

- Dedicate two-thirds of your cragging time (and days) to on-sight climbing.

- Pick on-sight routes with a rating from one number grade below to one letter above your hardest on-sight.

- Work redpoint routes up to one number grade beyond your hardest on-sight.

On-Sight Climbing Tips

Becoming a good on-sight climber is as much about what you do before the climb as it is about what you do on the route. Therefore, you can rapidly elevate your on-sight ability by optimizing your preclimb activities and rituals. Toward this end, let's look at six important strategies as used by top-shelf on-sight climbers.

Get Warmed and Primed

In a sense, on-sight climbing is like stepping into the ring with an unknown boxer. You don't know exactly what to expect until the fight's under way. You might get everything thrown at you right away, or it might not happen until the end—then, just when you feel you're in control, you get floored. Boxers know this and step into the ring only after performing a lengthy prefight warm-up that has every cell of the body primed to the max. Your preparations for an on-sight should have a similar effect—minus, of course, the profuse sweating of a prizefighter.

This lengthy comparison highlights an important fact—that many climbers fail on routes due to lack of proper warm-up. The ubiquitous flash pump is evidence of this. A properly warmed muscle will not pump out prior to the maximal exertion levels you're accustomed to from training. If you start the day fresh and perform a lengthy warm-up, you will never be surprised by an out-of-nowhere flash pump that sends you to the floor. Instead you'll know pretty much where you are with respect to pumping out and be able to attack the route in a suitable fashion.

Rico Thompson warming up on one of the many thin-pocketed faces at Wild Iris, Wyoming.

What's the best way to warm up for a serious on-sight attempt? Some gentle full-body stretching and sports massage of the fingers and forearms is a good start, but lots of submaximal climbing mileage is the ticket. Begin two number grades below your hardest on-sight and do about four one-pitch routes, each a little harder than the last. If 5.11c is your on-sight limit, start with a 5.9, followed by a 5.10a, then a 5.10c, ending with an easy 5.11. Take a twenty- to sixty-minute rest, and you'll be ready and primed for a great on-sight attempt. Most importantly, experiment to find out what works best for you in different situations. For example, when traditional climbing you might only have time for two warm-ups, whereas at a sport crag you might send up to six half-rope clip-ups before getting on the route of the day. No matter what your approach, it's fundamental that you avoid a vicious flash pump.

Scoping the Route

You only get one chance to on-sight a route. Scope it out like there's no tomorrow—because there isn't!

Clearly, a route well below your limit doesn't require much scoping other than determining issues of gear, safety, and maybe rest positions. But before you step onto a near-your-limit route, bag every bit of information available—just one minor detail overlooked might tip the scales against you. Always view the route from at least three different perspectives, not just straight-on from below as is common. Look for hidden holds in corners, around arêtes, above and below bulges, or anywhere else they might hide. Next, consider protection and clipping positions. Rack up your gear accordingly. Spend a lot of time determining every possible rest location and the best body position for each. Look for hand jams, knee locks, heel hooks, stems, and any small ledge you might be able to move laterally to reach. Of course, none of these rests is a "for-sure," but at least you know the possibilities and can attack the route appropriately.

The most obvious scoping concern is the sequence itself. The more angles and views you can get, the better. Is there a boulder or tree you can climb for a unique angle? Is there an easy route nearby you can climb to get a fair side view of the route? Maybe use binoculars to search for minor details. As you decipher the best-looking sequence, keep an open mind for alternative possibilities. You may want to memorize two sequences through the apparent crux section, then make the choice in person when you get there. Finally, don't get stuck in the bottom-up paradigm when figuring sequences. Often you can unlock a puzzling sequence by mentally downclimbing it from an obviously good hold or rest.

Your scope job may take anywhere from five minutes to an hour, depending on the complexity of the route. (Some climbers prefer to thoroughly scope and visualize a significant route for hours during a rest day.) Now that you've gathered all the data, it's time to preprogram a successful ascent with visualization.

Tips for Reading a Route

- Scope a route from at least three different perspectives, looking for hidden holds, rest positions, gear placements, and the best sequence.

- Climb a nearby boulder, tree, or even a by-the-side climb to gain a novel view of the route. Consider using binoculars.

- Decipher two conceivable sequences to any uncertain-looking sections.

- Use reverse sequencing to help solve puzzling sections.

Preprogramming the Ascent

Making the most of the data you've gathered requires vivid moviemaking via visualization. I'm not talking about a mental review of hold locations and order, the way many people (incorrectly) define the term *visualization* (what they're doing is simply mental rehearsal). Visualization, as used by top athletes around the world, is vivid, extremely detailed, full-color mental moviemaking—we're talking Steven Spielberg—which, through repetition, preprograms future reality in the brain!

After scoping your route, but before roping up, find a quiet out-of-the-way spot to sit or lie down for a few minutes. Relax and clear your mind of all other concerns (maybe run quickly through the Progressive Relaxation Sequence described on page 92). Begin recalling the images you "shot" earlier of the holds, location, order, rest, and gear. Blend them together into a moving picture. As you proceed, increase the brightness and detail of the movie to accentuate the preprogramming effect. Use all the visualization strategies listed on page 86.

Be careful not to program negatives or any uncertainty into your movies. If necessary, go back and rescope the climb to clarify the pictures or refigure a sequence. Then go back to your quiet spot and continue on with the visualization. Your ultimate goal is to learn the sequence, *feel* the moves and rest positions, and gain a strong sense of confidence in the upcoming ascent.

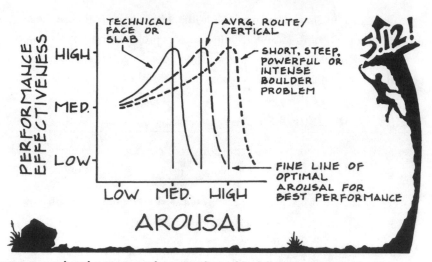

Lower arousal and a measured approach are ideal for thin, technical routes, whereas high arousal and a more aggressive attack are optimal for short, steep, powerful routes.

Optimizing Your Arousal

Arousal is your internal state of alertness or excitement. Your arousal is low when nodding off during your partner's pathetically slow leads and probably quite high when your last piece of gear pops out and slides down the rope. In climbing, arousal levels are in a constant state of flux, often determined by the pressure imposed by a given situation. As you react to each new situation, your awareness (or lack thereof) of changing arousal and your ability to control the arousal level has an enormous impact on your performance.

Ideal arousal levels in climbing relate to the physical and cognitive requirements of a route. The more complex the motor skills and sequence, the lower the optimal arousal level. For instance, a thin face climb demands pinpoint foot placements and complex sequencing, and thus is optimally performed in a calm, focused state. Conversely, a short, steep route of burly moves between big, obvious holds is best performed with vim and vigor. Of course, most climbs fall somewhere between these extremes and are best performed with moderate levels of arousal.

Your task is to determine the ideal arousal level for the route you plan to onsight, consciously preproduce that arousal, and then maintain it throughout the climb. Since most of us tend to be pretty psyched up before a big ascent, the most common situation is needing to moderate high arousal. Any thoughts that lower pressure or apprehension will help decrease arousal. Use the Progressive

Relaxation Sequence and ANSWER Sequence detailed in chapter 4 to further moderate arousal levels, the latter being your weapon of choice while climbing.

If you need to heighten your arousal level, start with some light physical activity to increase your heart rate and blood pressure (like some jumping jacks or a brief jog along the base of the cliff). Next, make your preclimb visualization overly bright, exaggerated, and moving at higher-than-usual speed. As a last resort, stimulants such as caffeine increase arousal—but also add to jitters and nervousness. In the end it comes down to your awareness and experience in a wide range of situations, and just knowing what's the right level for you.

Tips for Optimizing Arousal

- Determine the best level of arousal for each route. Create higher levels for powerful sequences and low to moderate arousal for the more technical and complex.

- Moderate arousal by supplanting outcome-oriented thinking with thoughts of preparing for the climb and the joy of the moment. Also, use the relaxation and centering sequences provided in chapter 4.

- Increase arousal using bright, loud visualization and through use of additional warm-up exercises. Some people find listening to music or consuming a caffeinated beverage an effective means of elevating arousal. Experiment to determine what works best for you.

Tactics Are Route-Dependent

There is no best on-sight strategy. Always tailor your tactics to the route at hand. If it's a thin route with dicey protection, you may need to sample the crux section by climbing up, then back down to a rest position (maybe several times), before trying it for real. On a powerful sport route, the best strategy may be an all-out blitzkrieg of going immediately with what looks right. Your typical approach will be somewhere between these extremes, although it's not uncommon to occasionally incorporate both on the same climb. As an example, you may be able to downclimb to the ground from an early crux then, after a rest, send it and the upper section with the blitzkrieg approach.

Your on-route rest tactics are critical as well. Program the location of all rest spots during your preclimb visualization. Don't hesitate to abandon a rest stance

Special tactics and tricks are often the key to sending routes near your limit. Here Nate Kimble catches a quick shakeout thanks to a knee lock on Cold War (5.14a), Waimea, Rumney, New Hampshire.
PHOTO: MIKE LANDKROON

and move on, however, if you find it takes more effort than it's worth. Keep an open mind to other rest possibilities—whether a novel knee bar or manky hand jam in a deep pocket. Even the slightest rest in the midst of a savage sequence just might save the day. Thus the bottom line in on-sighting: Be creative, ad-lib at will, and know when to rest and when to climb like there's no tomorrow.

Taking It to the Limit

The most powerful piece of information as you attempt an on-sight is *knowing* that the route goes! All the holds are there just waiting for you to unlock the order and physically put them together. A 100 percent belief that it can be climbed is tantamount to having it halfway in the bag.

A large percentage of would-be on-sighters fail because they never truly believe in a route. This is evident by their sloppy preclimb preparation or their namby-pamby effort ending in a "take" or "I can't do this." Conversely, the best on-sight climbers know it goes, and believe they have what it takes to do it, too. They plan meticulously, climb with creativity and intuition, and, when necessary, push aggressively through questionable moves and ominous crux sections. Bottom line: They succeed more often than not on their on-sights. And when they do fall, it's often sudden and with great surprise—surely they didn't expect to fall, they expected to flash!

So assuming the route is well protected and you have an alert belayer, always take your on-sight attempts to the limit. Use all the strategy and skill you have; put the pedal to the metal and empty the tank. Do this, and you'll win quite frequently, leaving fewer vendetta projects to come back to and redpoint.

Final On-Sight Tips

- Tailor your on-sight tactics to each route. Carefully read each climb and plan the best strategy based on your past experiences.

- Believe in the route! Even a fleeting doubt that it might not go is tantamount to adding a 10-pound weight to your back.

- Hold nothing back. You only get one chance to on-sight a route—so fall while trying, not while quitting.

Working a Redpoint Route

Working a redpoint is a game of strategy. And as in any game, the best players in our sport exhibit uncommon levels of thoughtfulness, patience, mental toughness, and resolve. In this section you will thus learn five techniques for fostering these abilities.

Get Data-Rich

Compared to the tight rules of on-sight climbing, working a redpoint is a veritable free-for-all of data-gathering and on-route tactics. The need for extensive preclimb scoping is much less urgent, because you get firsthand information as you work the route. Remember, in redpointing, the rope is a tool. Hanging and falling are a means to the end, while in on-sight climbing they are the end.

Before beginning work on the project, gather information from other climbers who have worked on or done the route. Don't worry about exact sequences yet; you may need or figure a different way anyhow. Instead focus on the basics of gear, rests, where the crux(es) is (are) located, and whether there are any hidden or "thank-God" holds. If there's no such beta available, take your best guess at it, then cast off up the route.

Your first goal is to hangdog up the entire route. The rope, gear, and your belayer are all fair tools to get you there. In fact, liberal use of the rope is advised to save vital energy you'll need later.

Chunking Down the Route

The benefits of chunking down a difficult climb into parts are both mental and physical. Psychologically, it reduces the burden of a long, hard route by allowing you to consider its parts as several shorter, doable climbs. Physically, chunking lets you dedicate full energy to solving the crux chunk first, as if it were a route of its own. Only when this is sent do you begin work on other easier parts of the climb.

Before you can chunk down the route, you need firsthand knowledge. Take a quick reconnaissance run up the climb to determine its logical parts—how you chunk down is, of course, route-dependent. For instance, a route made up of 70 feet of moderate climbing followed by just 10 hard feet to the top is best chunked in two parts. Knowing that the first 70-foot section is doable, get to work on solving and linking the last 10 feet while you're fresh. On a climb with multiple cruxes, chunk down each difficult section into a route of its own defined by good rest positions first and gear placements second. Sport climbers commonly break down routes bolt by bolt—for instance, a ten-bolt climb having ten chunks. After the first run through the route, grade each part (hardest, second hardest, easiest, and so forth) in your mind, considering that the upper parts may seem harder on redpoint due to fatigue. Always make solving the hardest part top priority.

Linking Chunks

The most popular method of linkage is to climb ever-increasing lengths of the route to the top. Consider the common scenario of working a route with the rope already through the top anchors. From the anchors, lower down the route (back-clip if overhanging) only as far as you think you can redpoint back to the top.

This might be only a 10-foot chunk if the end is the crux. If you succeed at that chunk, lower down and add another chunk to the linkup. Continue adding chunks until your starting point hits easy ground, or the actual ground. This process of linking chunks can take hours or days, depending on the length and difficulty of your project. But there's much greater value in this approach than in the old start-from-the-ground method.

Linking from top down makes you extremely familiar and confident in the final portion. On redpoint, it's here you want to be especially dialed in due to the accumulation of mental and physical fatigue. On the other hand, the from-the-ground approach commonly leaves you thrashing to refigure the top part, which you've practiced much less. Such ground-up efforts are more likely to result in a fall off the final moves, making a waste of even the most heroic effort.

Interlace Physical and Mental Practice

As you work chunks and begin linkage, incorporate extensive visualization into the process. After each fall, review and visualize the correct sequence. Use your rest

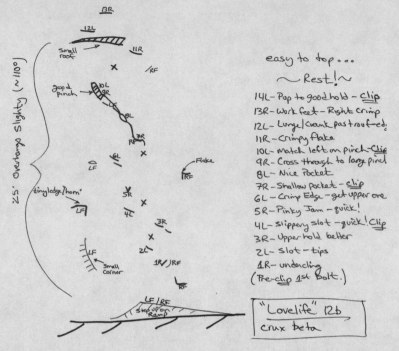

The handwritten beta sheet reads:

13R

12L

Small roof

11R

/RF

25' Overhangs slightly (~110°)

good pinch → 10L 9R

8L

7R RF

6L LF

Flake RF

tiny ledge / horn

5R LF

4C

3R

2C

1R/ /RF

Small corner LF

RF

LF /RF
Step up on Ramp

easy to top...

~ Rest !~

14L - Pop to good hold - clip
13R - Work feet - Right crimp
12L - Lunge / crank past roof-ed;
11R - Crimpy flake
10L - Match left on pinch - clip
9R - Cross through to large pinch
8L - Nice Pocket
7R - Shallow pocket - clip
6L - Crimp Edge - get upper one
5R - Pinky Jam - quick !
4L - slippery slot - quick ! clip
3R - Upper hold better
2L - Slot - tips
1R - undercling
(Pre-clip 1st Bolt.)

"Lovelife" 12b
crux beta

Create a beta sheet of your multiday project so you can train mentally during your rest days. Number all hand and foot placements and annotate key features or body positions.

time between tries to run some mental movies of the route. On multiday efforts, use rest-day visualization to aid memory of and further code the desired sequence. Prepare a beta map of long, complex routes to help guide your visualization.

This crib sheet should contain all hand- and footholds, rest positions, shakeouts, clips, or anything else that is a must to send the crux sequence. Number the order the holds are used, always specifying whether it's a left or right and a hand or foot placement. Write down descriptive words or names for critical holds to add detail and accuracy to your visualization. Annotations such as "sloping edge—get off it fast" or "solid pinch—good for a quick chalk-up" will really make things click on redpoint.

Build a Simulator

On a big project use your beta map to build a simulator of the crux section on a home wall or at a local gym. Many top climbers do this to train for projects, especially during the off season. An accurately built simulator develops motor skills and strength specific to the project, maintains move memory, and builds confidence.

Simulator training dates back at least to 1960, when John Gill began training for the small, pebbly Thimble route in the Needles of South Dakota. To simulate the difficult pebble pinching, Gill climbed the wall of a gymnasium by pinching nuts and bolts sticking out from the wall! Famous Colorado climber Jim Collins used route simulators to help train for cutting-edge, late 1970s ascents of Psycho Roof and Genesis. Undoubtedly, many of today's top climbers design their indoor training to simulate some project they are resolved to send. As you've learned in this book, specificity of training is everything, and route simulators are as specific as training gets. Consider building a simulator of your next serious project.

Tips for Working a Redpoint

- Obtain as much beta as possible from other climbers who have done the route. Inquire about gear, rest locations, hard-to-find holds, and where the hardest parts of the route are located.

- Begin with a reconnaissance run up the climb. Use the rope freely— hangdogging conserves energy. Learn the basics of the route and identify where the hard, moderate, and easy parts are located.

- Chunk down the route into believable parts. This is important, because a long, hard route carries a heavy burden when considered as a whole. Begin serious work on the hardest part first, then work the other chunks, ending with the easiest section.

- Linkage of the route should be done from the top down. For instance, link the last 20 feet to the top; if this is successful, rest and try to link the last 40 feet; and so on.

- Use visualization between attempts and on rest days. Prepare a beta map of complex sequences to guide accurate visualization and enhance move memory.

- Build an indoor simulator for serious, long-haul projects. Set a modular-hold copy of the crux sequence for the most specific training available other than climbing the route itself.

Sending Your Project

Tying in to the sharp end and sending your project is like stepping up to the free-throw line with the game on the line—telling yourself that you have to make it is a pressure-building, outcome-oriented mind-set that's often self-sabotaging. Peak performers (in anything) know that optimal execution is possible only when they are detached from possible outcomes and instead focused single-mindedly on the process or job at hand. In this section you will learn numerous strategies for preparing for and engaging your project as the most effective, efficient climber you can be.

Rest Long and Prosper

By nature, redpointing a route at the far reaches of your ability demands perfection. To maximize the odds of success, you need to be healthy, confident, well rested, and well warmed up. For a same-day attempt, take a double- to triple-length rest—whereas you normally rest about fifteen minutes between efforts, take about forty-five minutes before you go for the redpoint.

On a multiday route, take at least two rest days before attempting the redpoint. On the big day, get to the crag early and perform a long, gradual warm-up. You need to be mentally and physically primed to peak efficiency to send the route. This may mean several hours of warm-up climbing, stretching, and additional visualization. Kurt Smith tells how before redpointing his major project Slice of Life (5.13d) at Rifle, he sent as many as six routes in the 5.11 and 5.12 range. These were obviously climbs he had wired, but sending all six with ease prepared his mind and body for the big brawl.

Finally, for long-term projects worked over many weeks (possibly via simulator training), schedule the redpoint for the week following the end of a ten-week training cycle. (Remember, week ten is a full week off after the savage maximal-strength and anaerobic-endurance phases.) Upon completing this rest week, you will be stronger and more focused than at any time in the previous few weeks—the perfect time to redpoint your hardest-ever project.

Final Thoughts

Okay, you've worked it, visualized it, and linked all the hard parts. You are well rested, warmed, and primed like never before. Success or failure may now come down to your final thoughts as you step onto the rock. That's right: Just like a prizefighter stepping into the ring, you must believe 100 percent or else you're going down. Attempting a climb at your limit leaves no room for cruel doubts that will ultimately leave you hanging (on the rope).

Tune into your final thoughts after gearing up (shoes, harness, and so forth) and being put on belay. Close your eyes, take a few deep breaths, and relax throughout your body. Visualize successful execution of the route one final time. End this mental movie with the vision and feeling of successfully reaching the anchors, ledge, or clifftop. Now silence your mind by focusing on the feeling of air flowing in and out of your lungs. After a few slow, deep breaths, open your eyes and engage the rock with a calm, positive sense of knowing.

One Chunk at a Time

As you begin climbing, take the route one chunk at a time, whether that's bolt to bolt or rest to rest. (The burden of looking up and considering the route as a whole can be too great and may plant the seeds of failure in the form of jitters and doubts.) Mentally tick off each chunk as you complete it—this confidence builder will help propel you upward. Momentum will crescendo as you reach the upper part of the route, helping push you upward in the midst of increasing fatigue.

Living with Err—Or Air!

Some redpoint projects go easily, as you live out your mental movie and perform in the zone. Other times you make midroute errors such as botching a sequence—and maybe take air as the redpoint attempt comes to an abrupt end. No big deal! Remind yourself this is redpoint climbing, not on-sight. The rules are different, and errors and setbacks are part of the learning process.

Let's consider the case of a midroute error. You need to make a quick, often intuitive, call whether the error is a "fatal" or something you can live with and climb through. An example of a fatal error is botching a hand sequence, which leaves you with an impossible reach. In this case, drop onto the rope to conserve energy for another attempt. Before lowering to the ground, however, do the botched sequence one more time on toprope. Never start in the middle of a sequence (such as at the botched move); instead begin from the last break point and send the whole chunk. After doing this, visualize the correct sequence and run the mental movie a few more times as you rest on the ground.

Minor midroute errors are best accepted and dropped to the ground. Let's say that your foot pops off a hold, or you start to reach up with the wrong hand on a critical move. Instead of cursing the mistake, simply accept it as a reminder to renew your focus, then forget about it. To carry any thought of past errors is akin to carrying extra weight up the route.

Giving It Everything—Including Your Love

As in on-sight climbing, you cannot hold anything back when attempting a redpoint. Since the climb is at or beyond your known limits, 90 percent effort will not be enough. Throw everything you have at the rock—all your skill, experience, and strength as well as any tricks you are armed with. Hanging on the rope thinking "I could have tried harder" is a real bummer.

Interestingly, it's hard to give a climb 100 percent if you fear falling or feel you must send the route this attempt. Free yourself from this burden and lighten your mental load by deciding that you'll give it your best and love the route regardless of the outcome. By making this a core belief, you will dissolve the fear of failure that sabotages many climbers' performances and happiness.

Tips for Sending Your Project

- Don't rush into a redpoint attempt. Put in necessary work duty, then rest a lot. For a same-day redpoint try, triple your normal rest time between attempts. Consider taking a few rest days before going for the hardest projects.

- Final thoughts are key. Visualize a successful ascent of the entire route, then return to the present moment with a calm, positive sense of knowing. Step onto the rock confident, relaxed, and ready to enter the zone.

- Attack the route one chunk at a time, as if ticking off several doable boulder problems. Focus on the process of climbing each chunk and forget about the ultimate outcome.

- Learn to live with your mistakes. Climb through minor errors in sequence and forget about them immediately. If you commit a fatal error, hang on the rope and figure out what went wrong. Reclimb the problem chunk, then lower to the ground, rest, and visualize the correct solution.

- Hold nothing back and confidently go for it! Replace thoughts of the possible outcome with process-oriented thinking and unconditional love of the act of climbing.

Tricks for Tough Climbs

Whether redpoint or on-sight, it's often the clever fellows and gals who pull off the most brilliant ascents. Not *clever* as in "cheating without anyone knowing it," but in the sense of finding a hidden hold or new rest, or in the use of a trick move or special tactics on a given route. Now, while this book does not delve into teaching specific moves or techniques—personal one-on-one instruction is best for this—the focus here remains on presenting cutting-edge training techniques, the fundamental principles of climbing performance, and the must-know killer strategies needed to pursue 5.12 and beyond.

All of chapter 5 fits into the "killer strategies" category. This final section goes under the subhead of "trick" or "clever" tactics needed for the most insidious and continuous climbs.

Vary Grip Positions

The forearm muscles are almost always the critical point of failure when climbing at your limit. Thus any trick you can use to extend their life should be exploited. One of the best tricks is conscious cycling of grip position while climbing. This distributes accumulating stress over a wide range of muscular motor units.

Back in chapter 3 I explained how repeated use of the exact same grip position speeds up muscular failure. There is high training value in this approach (this is one reason HIT is so effective), but in operational situations, such as redpointing, it's the kiss of death. Instead of rapid muscular failure, you want long-lasting performance like the Energizer Bunny. Constant variation of grip use does just that it keeps you going and going and going . . .

Ultimately, each route dictates how far you can go with this strategy. For instance, a thin, edgy Smith Rocks route may limit you to cycling between crimp, open-hand, and an occasional thumb-lock grip. A pocketed Wild Iris route may allow use of all two- and three-finger teams, as well as some thumb presses and a jam or two in large pockets.

Finally, if your project requires several powerful open-hand pulls near the end of the route, avoid this grip down low in favor of the crimp grip. Thanks to specificity of grip strength, overuse of one grip position early on conserves contact strength in other positions for use later in the climb.

Trick moves, such as Sandy Litchfield's heel hook above the roof on #1 Super Guy (5.11b) at Shelf Road, can make a difficult move surprisingly casual.
PHOTO: STEWART GREEN

Focus on the Feet

"When the times get tough, focus on the feet." Remind yourself of this every time you begin to struggle on a route! Due to the proximity of the eyes to the hands, it's quite natural to overfocus on hand positioning at the expense of finding the best footholds. Ironically, the key to unlocking many routes lies in effective use of the feet. Consider how often you have fallen, only to notice a killer foot placement you missed.

Increasing focus on the feet takes practice and self-awareness. For starters, ask your belayer to yell at you to "look for feet" as you begin having difficulties on a route. The same thing goes in the gym or while bouldering. The more your attention is redirected toward finding the best footholds, the more automatic this will become in the future.

On difficult routes some climbers place small chalk tickmarks just above critical footholds as visual cues. This practice is quite effective when climbing fast is essential—still, you need to remember to look down in the first place! Consult chapter 4 to learn how to train for increased foot focus.

Climb Faster, Not Slower

Climbing too slow is one of the biggest errors in redpointing. Unlike on-sight, you know where all the holds, rests, and gear are located, so little time and thought need to be spent on these issues. When redpointing, in fact, you should climb as fast as possible without making technical errors.

Energy expenditure in climbing is proportionate to time—just as the longer Motel 6 "leaves the light on," the higher their electric bill. Since you have a finite amount of energy to send a route, it makes sense to get on and off small holds and through the crux sequence as fast as possible. Of course, blow a sequence by climbing sloppily and the energy-use issue is a moot point.

Cool your engines at the predetermined rest positions, then shift back into high gear as you climb into the next difficult section. Indeed, this goes against the conventional wisdom that says, "Proceed carefully in difficult times." While you might heed this "wisdom" on some on-sight or traditional routes, ignore it and climb faster on well-protected redpoint attempts.

Recover Faster with the G-Tox

The typical rest or break point on a redpoint is not a comfy stance you can camp out on forever. More commonly it's an okay handhold (you can match hands on it, if you're lucky) combined with a foot or lower-body position that takes significant weight off the arms. A few seconds to a couple of minutes later, the "rest" may become an energy drain—it begins to take more energy to remain there than you recover. A smart climber is out of there by this point of diminishing returns.

Knowing when you've reached this critical point comes from experience redpointing and anaerobic-endurance interval training. Assuming that you know how long to stay at a rest, the goal becomes doing anything to maximize recovery (detoxing the forearms is the main concern) during the respite. The normal protocol for recovery at marginal midclimb rests is relaxed breathing and shaking out the arms. As we all know, this yields noticeable recovery. Back around 1990, however, I developed a midclimb shaking-out strategy that fosters even greater recovery. I call it the G-Tox.

The G-Tox is only slightly different from the shakeout described above. In it you alternate the position of the shakeout arm between the normal down position and a raised-hand position (as in school). The regimen I find works best is five to ten seconds with the arm above your head, followed by five to ten seconds in the down position. Keep repeating this until you sense you're near the point of diminishing returns, then get climbing.

My G-Tox method works better than the normal shakeout by using gravity to its advantage. During use of the normal hands-down shakeout, blood pools in the forearms (the pump you feel and see), due partially to gravity's hindrance of venous return flow toward the heart. Addition of the raised-hand position uses gravity to enhance venous return of "used" blood out of the arm. This return flow takes some lactic acid with it and allows more fresh, oxygenated blood to enter. The end result is greater recovery in the same amount of time as the old standard method. (How much extra is hard to say, but even a modest 10 or 20 percent gain is significant when climbing at your limit.) More and more top climbers are starting to use the G-Tox—it's time for you to give it a try, too!

Boone Speed detoxing in the midst of Malvado at American Fork, Utah. You can speed midroute recovery by using the G-Tox at such rests. Alternate the position of the resting arm between the down position (pictured) and a raised-hand position. PHOTO: STEWART GREEN

Tips on Tricks

- Cycle your grip over the widest range of possible positions to spread out fatigue. Or if you know you need full power of a specific grip for the crux, avoid its use up to that point.

- When the going gets tough, focus on the feet. Of course, try to pay constant attention to finding the best footholds—the legs are stronger than the arms.

- Climb faster, not slower, through difficult sequences to conserve energy.

- Use the G-Tox to enhance recovery on those all-too-brief marginal shakeouts. Alternate your resting arm between the raised-hand and the dangling-by-the-side position, shaking it slightly for five to ten seconds in each position. Repeat this process as long as the rest stance allows.

Eric Hörst on Sling Time (5.11d),
Shawangunks, New York.

CHAPTER SIX

Frequently Asked Questions

All that you throw at the rock comes back into yourself. You become the result of your struggles, the
sum of your efforts. —Todd Skinner

M y goal in writing *How to Climb 5.12* was to craft a streamlined, content-rich book covering only the most vital topics relating to climbing performance. Applying the material presented in the first five chapters will help propel you to higher levels of performance and, if you desire, to 5.12 and beyond.

In this final chapter I will touch on a few topics that climbers I meet at the crags, training seminars, and through my Web site regularly query. It's likely you have also pondered some of these same questions, and I invite you to e-mail me with a question of your own. Please make your question as specific as possible and e-mail it to question@TrainingForClimbing.com. Though I can't guarantee a quick reply, I do attempt to respond to each and every e-mail I receive.

What It Takes to Climb 5.12

Q: It seems that most people doing routes of 5.12 and harder climb full time. Although I've been climbing less than a year, I desperately want to crank at that level. Do I need to quit my job, sell my house, and become a climbing bum to make the grade?

Keep your job and house, and put in a few more years of regular climbing and focused training. Chances are 5.12 is well within your reach without a major upheaval in your life.

Thousands of people climb 5.12 and have a "normal" life. I know of countless teachers, managers, lawyers, salesmen and -women, contractors, doctors, home keepers, business owners, and full-time students who regularly climb 5.12 as weekend warriors. The key ingredients common to all these individuals are a dedication to train hard and intelligently for a couple of days each week and a willingness to travel many weekends to pull down on some good rock.

The weekday training must be specific to climbing—forget the local health club. Join a climbing gym and, if possible, build a home wall. A small, steep

Fifty-something climber Cindy Ann Hintz and her husband, Charles Ganote (a sixty-year-old forensic pathologist), both climb 5.12 as weekend warriors. Here Cindy warms up on She Rides (5.9), Bubba City, New River Gorge, West Virginia.

home wall makes a good workout possible on even the most hectic days. An hour of bouldering on an overhanging wall trains the strength, the endurance, and many of the techniques you'll need in your quest for the twelfth grade.

On weekends, travel, travel, travel. It's important to get experience on many different kinds of rock, so don't lock in to spending every weekend at the same (closest) crag. Dedicate Saturday to working on a couple of project routes, then climb for mileage (practice) on Sunday.

Finally, long-term gains require consistent and congruent actions. Plan your workout and travel schedule as far into the future as possible—ad-lib workouts won't cut it. Neither will activities that run counter to the nine absolutes (see chapter 1). Whether it's excessive training or excessive partying, your climbing will suffer and you'll come up short of your goals.

So for now, stay the course. Train smart, climb hard, and drop me a note when you send your first 5.12!

Tip: Your quest for 5.12 must be based on a sound strategy and disciplined day-to-day actions. Train and climb up to a total of four days per week, and avoid activities that run counter to your fitness and climbing goals. Constantly stretch your abilities and hone your strategy—you'll be knocking on the door to 5.12 sooner than you expect.

Optimal Climbing and Rest Schedule

Q: While on a road trip, how many days per week can I climb without seeing a major drop-off in performance or risking an overuse injury?

Four days of climbing per week is a good number for planning purposes, but you'll want to adjust the actual number according to your amount of sleep, quality of nutrition, and intensity of climbing. Assuming reasonable sleep and diet habits, the number of rest days should be in direct proportion to the intensity of your climbing.

High-end climbers frequently take two days off after a single day of maximal effort on a cutting-edge project. Extreme physical efforts require extended recovery. If attempting (or training for) a severe redpoint, you might climb as little as two or three days per week.

More typical of a road trip is the desire to pack in lots of climbing near or just below your limit. When I'm on trips, I place greater value on sending lots of 5.12s as opposed to spending a week on a single superhard project. Many others agree with this approach, making a schedule of two days on, one day off, two days on, two days off quite popular. You'll get in four good days of climbing per week along with enough rest to help prevent overuse injuries and maintain performance level.

When alpine or big-wall climbing, you may be able to survive on just one or two rest days per week. By today's cragging standards many alpine routes are quite moderate, making for a workout higher in volume than intensity. Similarly, mixed climbing on big walls involves lots of hanging around and relatively easy free climbing. Of course, there are other variables that can complicate matters in these settings, including lack of food and water, high altitude, and poor weather. Ultimately, awareness of the situation and yourself must dictate the schedule.

As a final note, when sport climbing it's best to avoid climbing more than two consecutive days. Repeating the same stressful moves and sequences—as in working a route—is especially hard on the tendons, muscles, and nervous system. Three or more straight days of this type of climbing will eventually lead to a decline in performance and possibly injury. Use an every-other-day climbing schedule or the two-on, one-off, two-on, two-off schedule presented above.

Tip: Take rest days in proportion to the intensity of your climbing. Two days of rest per week may suffice when climbing moderate alpine or big-wall routes. Peak performance on high-end climbs may require two or three days off for each single day of high-intensity climbing. As a rule, avoid cragging more than two consecutive days.

The Effects of Indoor Climbing on Real-Rock Performance

Q: Is it true that indoor climbing can hurt outdoor, real-rock performance?

Yes and no! To explain my answer, let's consider the pros and cons of indoor climbing. First the pros, which clearly outweigh the cons. Indoor walls bring climbing closer to where we live, allowing for more regular practice of skills. Bouldering caves and home walls offer excellent sport-specific training for the fingers, upper body, and core muscles of the torso. Artificial walls can (and have) given birth to new moves that are also useful on real-rock climbing. And pulling down indoors is a fun rainy-day alternative to climbing outside (important in the East!).

Now for the main drawback of indoor walls: They are generally a poor representation of real rock. While most of the moves and techniques are the same as used outdoors, the holds, texture, and terrain are very different. This greatly limits transfer of skill from human-made to real rock—hence the "yes" portion

Indoor climbing is great training, but it's vital that you keep it real by climbing outside on as wide a range of rock types as possible. Here Lisa and Eric Hörst enjoy the classic Book of Solemnity (5.10a), Cathedral Ledge, New Hampshire.

PHOTO: STEWART GREEN

of my answer. Excessive indoor climbing commonly leads to lackluster footwork at the crags. Real-rock footholds are harder to spot and use, and their frictional properties are less predictable. In addition, no indoor wall can prepare you for the variety of techniques you'll need to excel outside.

Don't get me wrong; I'm a huge advocate of commercial climbing gyms, and I love my home wall! Indoor climbing has tremendous training value, and it's great fun. Still, if real-rock climbing is your goal, you must get out on the real stuff regularly to maintain your form and technique and gain real-world experience.

Tip: Use indoor walls as a supplement to outdoor climbing—not the reverse. For optimal results, combine high-intensity indoor bouldering and interval training on routes to build strength with high-mileage days on real rock to train endurance and technique.

Fingerboard-Training Tips

Q: There are no crags or climbing gyms nearby, nor do I have space to build a home wall. I've decided to buy a fingerboard, and I'm wondering what type of training is best.

A fingerboard is an effective tool for training maximum grip strength, pulling power, and lock-off strength. Two brief, high-intensity workouts per week will help improve sport-specific strength with minimal risk of injury. At the same time, many overzealous individuals have trained too long and too often, and sadly many have ended up with finger, elbow, or shoulder injuries. Here is a blueprint for a safe, effective fingerboard workout.

Perform your fingerboard training according to the four requirements for effective maximal finger-strength training as discussed in chapter 3. Let's recap the four training requirements:

1. Train at near-maximal intensity throughout the set.

2. Produce muscular failure in less than one minute.

3. Use movements and body positions specific to climbing.

4. Focus on and "fry" a single grip position for an entire set.

Well-designed fingerboard workouts can meet three of these four requirements. Still, you'll come up short in the category of "movements and positions specific to climbing." Oh well, let's make the most of it. Here's how.

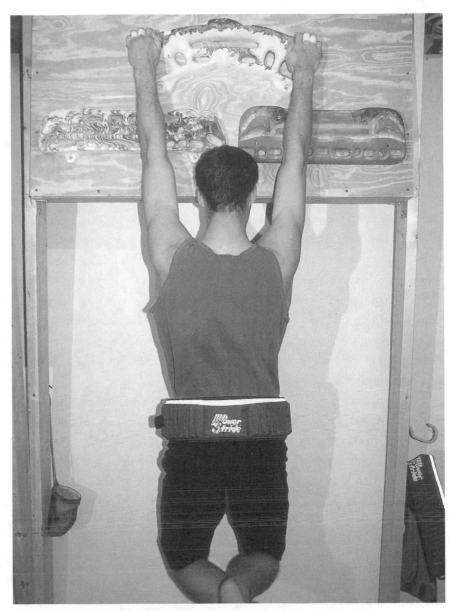

Brief, high-intensity hangs on a fingerboard develop finger strength. Here a weight belt is being used to increase the difficulty and simulate hypergravity.

Begin with a slow warm-up of at least fifteen minutes. A few minutes of light aerobic activity (such as jogging or jumping rope) is ideal, though not mandatory. Some gentle stretching of the upper body is important, however (see chapter 3 for specific stretches). Alternate stretching exercises with a few sets of pull-ups performed on the fingerboard's largest holds. Finish up with some self-massage of the fingers and forearms. The meat of your finger-strength training should be a series of repeaters. Keep your arms nearly straight and favor small- to medium-sized, reasonably comfortable holds. Avoid tweaky, sharp holds like the local sandbagger, and resist training on the one-finger pocket holds until you reach 5.12 (you'll have something to look forward to!).

Repeaters involve six maximum-intensity hangs on the same pair of holds. Each hang must last only three to ten seconds, followed by a rest of exactly five seconds (buy a stopwatch and be exact). The whole set takes just over a minute. Now take a one-minute rest before beginning one more set on the same pair of holds. Rest again for one more minute, then move on to another set of holds. Work your problem grips first (for me, this is pinches), then progress from smaller to larger holds as you tire. Beginners should work only six grips (twelve sets of repeaters), whereas advanced people can work ten grips for a total of twenty sets. Finally, it's important to add weight to your body when working any fingerboard grips on which you can hang for more than ten seconds. Start with 5 pounds added to your harness and increase the weight gradually over several weeks. Better yet, buy a 10- and a 20-pound weight belt, or add 2-pound diver's weights in a fanny pack. This way you can add or subtract weight quickly between sets.

Upon completing your repeaters, rest for a few minutes then finish up your workout with two to five sets of pull-ups. Your goal is ten to fifteen pull-ups per set. If you can't do this many, don't skip over them! Instead have someone act as a spotter, helping lift (grabbing around your hips) as much weight as needed so that you can do between five and ten pull-ups. Use this strategy three days per week and you will soon be doing the pull-ups on your own. Conversely, you must add 10 to 20 pounds of extra resistance (using a weight belt) if you can do more than fifteen pull-ups. Rest for three minutes between sets.

Vitamin Supplements for Climbers

Q: What vitamin or herbal supplements might I take to help enhance my physical performance?

No vitamin or herbal supplement can enhance performance anywhere near as much as a solid training and climbing program combined with quality rest and nutrition. Unless you're doing all these things right, invest your money in climbing trips or the stock market—you'll get better performance either way. If you are training according to the absolutes and principles discussed earlier, however, you may benefit from the handful of supplements that are both proven to work and legal. If that's you, here's what to consider when you go shopping.

Start by reminding yourself that most of the things vitamin and herbal companies tell you are pseudoscientific half truths or, in some cases, outright lies. The fact is that most of the supplements on the market don't have a shred of evidence to back up the grandiose claims made for them. What's more, ignore the testimonials of famous athletes (who have genetics and years of training to thank for their success), which are merely anecdotal and carry no scientific weight. Look for products with some scientific backing, ideally in the form of double-blind, placebo-controlled studies (and results published in peer-review journals). Here are a few such supplements proven useful for serious athletes. You'll need to decide for yourself whether they're worth your money.

More than one hundred studies have shown that antioxidants prevent muscle damage and shorten recovery time. Although half a dozen different antioxidants work toward this end, I suggest vitamins C and E and selenium—they are synergistic and quite affordable. Buy the cheapest (generic) brands you can find, since when it comes to these vitamins they are all basically the same. As for how much to take, total daily supplementation of 1 gram of vitamin C, 400 International Units of vitamin E, and 100 micrograms of selenium split into two doses (morning and evening) will suffice. Individuals training at extremely high intensities and volumes can safely double these amounts.

Next, consider supplementing your protein intake. If you are not consuming enough protein, your body may be cannibalizing muscle, especially during long workouts or days of climbing. As with the antioxidants above, the recommended dietary allowance (RDA) for protein is far too low for hard-training athletes. Numerous studies have shown the need for between 1.0 and 1.5 grams of protein per kilogram of body weight per day to maintain positive nitrogen balance in athletes. For a 150-pound climber, this translates to between 70 and 100 grams per day—surely a difficult amount to eat without loading up on fattening dairy products and meat. Enter whey protein powder, which mixes easily with water, juice, or skim milk to make for a high-quality, easily digestible protein supplement.

Until a few years ago, many protein mixes contained low-quality soy protein and were packed with carbohydrates. Much has changed since then. Today there are several brands of high-quality whey protein available from General Nutrition Center (GNC) or by mail order. Specifically, look for brands containing "lactose-free whey peptides." This form of protein maintains nitrogen balance longer and possesses higher biological value than lean meat, chicken, fish, milk, or any other protein source! Drinking a glass of whey protein first thing in the morning, after an intense workout, and before bed thus gives your body what it needs to rebuild itself stronger and recover faster.

Herbs, homeopathic supplements, and Eastern medical treatments are the latest rage with many athletes. While these nontraditional supplements and practices are intriguing and generally harmless, they continue to be highly controversial in the scientific community. Clearly, there is little research to support the claimed benefits of many homeopathic products. While this does not mean that they definitively do not work, it should make any thinking person ponder the validity of any herbal product before ponying up any hard-earned money for the latest "in" concoction.

Tip: Purchase only supplements backed by legitimate scientific research. When in doubt, save your money. I do strongly endorse taking a daily multivitamin and the use of whey protein powder as a dietary supplement. Hard-training climbers will benefit from taking the proven antioxidants—vitamins C and E and the mineral selenium.

Nutrition Tips to Enhance Performance and Accelerate Recovery

Q: I have heard a lot of talk about a new scale for classifying the energy release of different foods called the glycemic index. What is this index and of what use is it to climbers?

Consumption of high-glycemic-index foods elicits a rapid increase in blood sugar and then a large insulin response. Low-glycemic-index foods produce more subtle variations. Climbers can use knowledge of the glycemic index (GI) to control energy levels and to speed recovery after a workout. Here's how.

Stable insulin levels are optimal for long-duration activities such as climbing, hiking, and long training sessions. It's been shown that a steady insulin level supports steady energy and steady thinking (focus) while discouraging fat storage. This makes low- to medium-index foods preferable for climbers most of the time. Conversely, high-GI foods produce large swings in blood sugar and an insulin spike. One minute you are Jonesing to crank another hard route, and the next you are yawning and ready to call it a day. A climber serious about performance would therefore be wise to avoid high-GI foods and beverages while on the rock or in the gym. The exception is the two hours immediately following your workout—more on this in a bit.

Figuring the glycemic index of certain foods is more difficult than it might seem at first. For instance, most foods classified as simple carbohydrates (candy, cookies, some fruit juices, and most sports drinks) are high-GI foods. So are potatoes, white rice, bread, and bagels, however—all generally considered complex carbohydrates. Low-GI foods include vegetables, whole grains, brown rice, milk, and most high-protein energy bars or balanced-style energy bars (see table). As a general rule, the more processed and easily digestible a food, the higher its glycemic index (for example, liquids have higher index than similar food solids). High-fiber foods tend to elicit a slower insulin response and thus have a low GI. Finally, foods containing some protein and fat along with carbohydrates come in lower on the scale, too.

Glycemic Index of Common Foods

HIGH (> 70)		MEDIUM (50–69)		LOW (< 50)	
Bagel	72	Banana	~55	Bulgur	48
Carrots	71	Bran Muffin	60	Spaghetti	41
Corn Chips	73	Oatmeal	61	Whole Wheat	37
Cornflakes	77	Raisins	64	All Bran	42
Doughnut	76	Rice	56	Orange	43
Honey	73	Sweet Potato	54	Pear	36
Jelly Beans	80	Wheat Crackers	67	Apple	38
Potatoes	83	Cookies	~60	Peas	48
Rice (instant)	91	Sucrose	65	Baked Beans	48
Rice Cakes	82	Soft Drinks	68	Lentils	29
Rice Krispies	82	Orange Juice	57	Milk (Skim)	32
Grape-Nut Flakes	80	Granola Bars	61	Fructose	23
Cracker (Soda or Water)	~76	Macaroni	64	Grapefruit	23
Glucose	100	Shredded Wheat	58	Yogurt (w/ Fruit)	~30
Gatorade	78	Ice Cream	~60	Peanuts	14

This last piece of information is useful if you don't have the gumption to memorize and use this index. Consuming some protein and a little fat during each of your carbohydrate feedings serves to moderate the overall glycemic response of the meal. So for a long day at the crags, pack some fruit, a couple of balanced-style energy bars, and a fructose-based sports drink that contains some protein (if you can find one).

As mentioned earlier, the one good time to consume high-glycemic-index foods—such as candy, juice, soda pop, and quick-energy sports drinks like Gatorade—is at the end of your workout or day of climbing. Intense exercise primes the muscles to immediately reload energy reserves in the form of glycogen. High blood sugar and the insulin spike help drive this repletion process. The optimal window for these high-GI foods is the first two hours following exercise. After that, favor low- to medium-index foods for slow, steady refueling.

You can best accelerate recovery by consuming a snack or drink with a four-to-one ratio of carbohydrate to protein during the crucial two-hour postworkout recovery window. Upon concluding a day at the crags, you might eat a high-protein energy bar and drink a quart of Gatorade, or you could consume a four-to-one sports drink. At home it would be best to consume a few glasses of juice or other sucrose-based drink and chase it with a serving of whey protein drink. In the next hour or two, partake in a well-balanced meal comprised of a 65–15–20 percent total caloric breakdown of carbohydrate, protein, and fat.

Tip: Choose low- to medium-glycemic-index foods as the foundation of your diet to provide sustained energy throughout the day. Ideal foods to take climbing are fruit, balanced-style energy bars, and a sports drink that contains some protein. Reserve high-index foods for consumption immediately after training and climbing to help speed repletion of energy stores. Research has shown that you can accelerate recovery by as much as 50 percent by consuming a four-to-one carbohydrate-to-protein sports drink in the two hours after cessation of exercise (the sooner, the better).

The Importance of Downtime and the Reminiscence Effect

Q: Is it necessary to take time off from climbing? I know a few people who break from climbing for a month or more, claiming it helps their performance! Wouldn't climbing year-round maximize technical and physical gains?

No, climbing year-round is not a good practice; and yes, a month off can help your climbing! I qualify this answer by adding that it applies to those who climb at least twice per week, consistently throughout the year.

The grind of climbing several days per week over the long term takes a mental and physical toll. For instance, motivation and absolute performance level often flatten out or decline after a few consecutive training cycles or a long road trip. Worse yet, trying to break the plateau by training harder (per conventional wisdom) can produce even greater negative effects. Taking some time off is the fastest way back on track and, ironically, may be the answer to stale climbing or a long-term plateau.

One month totally away from climbing—no gym climbing, no home walls, no sport-specific training—during the off season can yield great results. Sure, you'll lose a few percentage points of your strength, but that will return quickly upon resumption of training and climbing. What's more important is that your renewed motivation and refreshed neuromuscular system may rapidly give birth to new levels of training and climbing performance!

Physically, this downtime benefits you in two ways. First, it will nip in the bud any nagging or underlying injuries. Several weeks off will finally give your tendons the time necessary to repair and strengthen to a new level, making them more resistant to injury as you return to pursue even higher grades. Your muscles also rebound, because they finally get an extended recovery break. Accumulated fatigue from several training cycles may unknowingly have you on the verge of overtraining. If that's you, expect your strength to rebound after three or four weeks of rest from the use and abuse.

The second benefit of occasional time off is a fascinating phenomenon called reminiscence. This long-known effect is based on the fact that your body remembers more about complex skills (call it muscle memory) than does your conscious mind. Long bouts of regular climbing can leave you trying too hard, overanalyzing situations, and possibly too outcome-oriented. Your climbing movements may begin feeling awkward and forced, and your performance curve may straight-line due to central fatigue—that is, fatigue of the nervous system. Eventually, you'll be wondering, "Why isn't all this practice time making me better?" or, "Why do I suddenly feel off keel and uncoordinated on the rock?"

Time away from climbing will clear your head, allow your nervous system to recover (which can take up to seven times longer than recovery of the muscle itself), and reset your intuitive sense of movement. Greeting your return to the rock will be more automatic and natural movement as your body remembers (reminisces) the well-learned motor skills of climbing. This "try-softer" style will not overpower your body's knowledge of the skills the way the old try-harder approach did. You'll be pleasantly surprised to find yourself climbing better, more efficiently, and with more flow than before. This powerful reminiscence effect has been experienced time and time again by participants in many sports ranging from golf to gymnastics. So the next time your climbing stagnates, take a month off and let your body remember how to climb.

Tip: If you are serious about climbing your best, commit to taking one month off from climbing each year. That's right. Such downtime will renew motivation, allow any nagging injuries to heal, and enable the nervous system to recover from a long stretch of hard climbing (and training). Upon returning to the rock, you'll also find yourself feeling more dialed in and intuitive thanks to the powerful reminiscence effect. Note: Individuals climbing and training less than a total of eight days per month may not experience this effect.

Treatment of the Common Finger Tendon A2 Pulley Injury

Q: I just tweaked a tendon near the base of my left ring finger. Can I climb through this injury or should I take some time off?

The short answer is to stop climbing and give the finger a few weeks of complete rest. Do this, and hopefully you'll prevent it from becoming a chronic injury.

Injury to the A2 tendon pulley at the base of the finger is ubiquitous among climbers. It can happen on a single strenuous move or over the course of many weeks. But once you've gotten it, this insidious injury can linger for months, especially if you try to climb through it. Time off is the only sure cure. A preemptive strike of a month off will usually arrest the condition.

Granted, few climbers have the patience to take a full month off. Still, noted climber and orthopedic surgeon Dr. Mark Robinson urges you to heed severe tendon pangs and swelling early on and embark on the following course of action:

1. Cease climbing until all pain and swelling are gone (maybe only a week or two if you catch it early).

2. Take two more weeks off.

3. Perform two weeks of low-resistance finger and hand exercises using squeeze devices, finger putty, and dumbbells.

4. Begin climbing on large-hold routes for up to one month.

5. Move on to large-hold steep routes such as cave bouldering and such for one month, then back to full-force climbing thereafter.

Frequent icing and use of anti-inflammatory medicines early on (while swelling persists) may speed healing, but use beyond the first few weeks is of little value. This complete course of action may take up to six months in severe cases. It is, however, a great investment in your long-term climbing health and capabilities. Return to climbing too soon and a series of recurrences is likely.

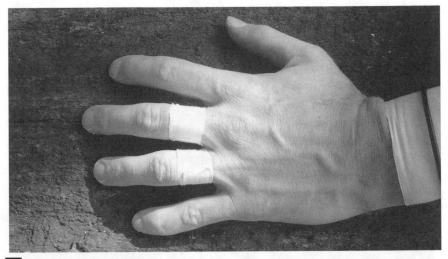

1. Ring method—Wrap three firm turns of tape around the base of the finger to support the A2 pulley.

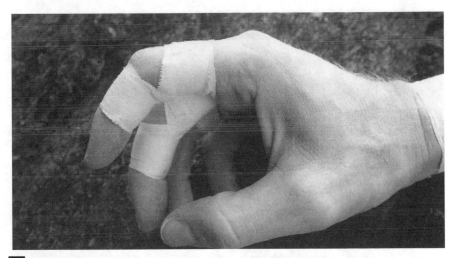

2. X method—Use this method to provide skin protection, in addition to supporting the A2 pulley. With a slight bend in the finger, begin with two turns of tape around the base of the finger. Continue under the middle joint and take two turns around the middle of the finger, then pass back over the bent middle joint and conclude with a final loop around the base of the finger.

As you return to climbing, reinforce the injured finger with tape. A few snug turns of athletic tape around the base of the finger helps support the injured tendon and presumably decreases the chance of reinjury. Finally, the myth that anti-inflammatories (for example, ibuprofen and aspirin) taken before climbing helps prevent finger injuries is false—it can do just the opposite.

Tip: Stop climbing until pain and swelling are gone, then take two more weeks off. Begin with light resistance training for two weeks, then start climbing on big-hold easy climbs (at least two number grades below your redpoint level) for one month. Progress to more difficult climbs during the next month, then full-force climbing beyond that if you're still symptom free.

Building an Affordable Home Training Wall

Q: I'd like to build a home training wall. What is the most affordable, effective, and easy design to build?

An 8-by-12-foot 45-degree overhanging wall is an effective bare-bones rig. I know of many such walls built in dorm rooms, apartments, basements, garages, attics, and backyards. Vertical climbing distance is less important than steepness. Savage three- to six-move problems are all you need to build power. Link up a

A small home wall can provide a great workout and some really good times. Here's a typical overhanging wall constructed in a small apartment in Colorado.

few of these problems to train anaerobic endurance. Voilà, a sport-specific workout in the comfort of your home!

Holds are important. Don't skimp on real rock—go for plastic. You'll thank God you did after just a few workouts! Seriously, the holds on your wall play a major role in how often and long you train. To start, buy a variety of holds from several companies to see what you like. Then just load up your wall with as many holds as you can fit in! Select holds with a fine texture (or use sandpaper to smooth high-texture holds) so your skin does not wear out before your muscles.

Since your wall is steep, favor medium-sized shapes with usable features while avoiding highly detailed holds with many small edges (merely bells and whistles). Add some well-rounded pockets and small yet comfy crimp edges for working contact strength. As a guideline, select hold sizes as follows: 10 percent tiny foot chips (real rock is okay here), 20 percent small crimp edges, 30 percent pockets, 30 percent a variety of medium-sized holds and pinches, and 10 percent large buckets.

If space and finances allow, consider adding a couple of other wall angles to your home gym. I suggest incorporating a few panels that are 20 to 30 degrees past vertical, as well as a flat roof section. Be creative and have fun with your design, but avoid 90-degree angles and minimize square footage of vertical wall space.

Now recruit a few good training partners and develop a sound, intelligent training program. In addition to your muscles, it's vital to also exercise self-discipline—don't get sucked into using your wall daily. Climbing more than four days per week is a road to ruin. Train hard and smart—and have fun!

The Truth about Campus Training

Q: I would like to add some campus training to my workout, but I've heard it's dangerous. What type of regimen do you suggest and how do I avoid getting injured?

There are two basic styles of campus training: the no-feet climbing up an overhanging wall with modular holds, and the dynamic up-and-down style performed on a specialized campus board. The first style is a diluted form of campus training, and it's what I advise for intermediate climbers wishing to experiment with campus training. The extremely dynamic latter method should be used only by the most well-conditioned elite climbers. Let's first look at the less stressful, though still difficult no-feet campus training on an overhanging modular wall.

The goal here is maximal-intensity, no-feet boulder problems up a 45-degree overhanging wall. Three- to ten-move problems are ideal. Start in a sitdown position and end on a good hold that clearly defines the end. This type of campus training will develop contact strength, upper-body power, and lock-off strength.

Up-campusing on a modular wall is less stressful and provides more variation in training grips and power.

Begin with a comprehensive twenty- to forty-minute warm-up composed of stretching, self-massage of the fingers and forearms, a few sets of pull-ups, and general bouldering. Crescendo bouldering intensity as you near the end of the warm-up period, then take a five- to ten-minute rest.

The meat of your workout is ten to thirty campus routes (as defined above). Each route or attempt lasts only a few seconds, but always take a two-minute rest after each. This part of your workout will last between twenty-five and sixty minutes. Your first few routes should be "gimmes" up a series of five to eight large holds. The next five to twenty routes (or attempts) should be new and maximal.

If you fail on the first attempt, try it up to three more times (always resting two minutes between attempts). If you still have no success, memorize the route to try during your next workout and move on. Wind down your campus workout with a few more campus problems of decreasing difficulty. Now is the time to attempt flashes of some of your favorite campus problems (wired) from past workouts. End the session when you begin to fail on easy or wired routes. Flogging yourself beyond this point has little training value, courts injury, and digs a deeper hole from which you must recover before you can train again.

Now let's look at the original style of campus training as developed by Wolfgang Güllich. This is the highly impressive dynamic up-and-down, double-hand campus training that's been featured in numerous videos. While not quite as difficult as it first appears, this explosive exercise is extremely stressful and best left to elite climbers.

Begin by hanging straight-armed from the second or third rung of a wooden campus board. Let go with both hands simultaneously, dropping down to catch

Hanging start

Drop down

Double dynos on a specialized campus board are the gold standard for developing power and contact strength. . . .

Catch lower rung

Explode back up to catch starting rung.

. . . Still, only healthy, elite climbers should perform this highly stressful type of training.

the bottom rung then immediately exploding back up to the starting rung. Without hesitation drop down again, catch, and explode back up. Continue in this fashion until you fail to make one of the catches. Depending on the size of the rungs used, you may achieve anywhere from one to ten drop-down-and-explode-up reps (one full cycle). Rest for five minutes before considering another set. Remember that when training near your limit, there is a fine line you must not cross—err on the side of doing too few sets instead of too many. End your campus workout immediately at the first sign of pain in the fingers, elbows, or shoulders. Cool down with some upper-body stretching and two sets of reverse wrist curls.

Tips for Campus Training

- Engage in campus training only if you are an advanced climber (able to toprope 5.12a or harder) with at least two years of sport-specific training under your belt, and no recent history of finger or arm injuries.

- Warm up thoroughly; this should include about thirty minutes of progressively more difficult bouldering. Consider reinforcing the base of your fingers with a few tight turns of half-inch athletic tape.

- Emphasize quality over quantity. Five quality sets on the campus board is better than ten sloppy, poorly executed sets. Remember, campus training is only a small portion of a good strength-training workout—don't treat it as if it's the only method of training for climbing.

- Do not campus train while in a state of high fatigue—it's vital to maintain good technique and high-quality execution (for instance, not catching with completely straight arms).

- End the training session immediately upon any sign of joint or tendon pain.

- Rest for a minimum of two days after a serious campus-training workout. Limit yourself to two modest-length sessions per week, and cycle two weeks on and two weeks off.

Lowering Injury Risk

Q: So many climbers I know are walking wounded with nagging injuries in their shoulder, elbow, fingers, or elsewhere. What can I do to prevent getting injured?

The only way to absolutely prevent climbing injury is to *not climb*. Of course, that isn't an option for rock addicts like us, so let's look at seven strategies for lowering injury risk.

Always Warm Up and Cool Down

Anyone with experience in traditional sports knows firsthand the importance of a proper warm-up and cool-down. Unfortunately, I have observed more than a few climbers who just tie in and start climbing without any preparatory warm-up activity, stretching, or submaximal climbing.

All that's needed for a good warm-up is to break a light sweat by jogging, hiking, or riding a bike for five to fifteen minutes. Follow this with some light stretching exercises (see chapter 3). Start your climbing for the day by doing a series of easy boulder problems or a route or two that is much easier than you might want to get on. This minor inconvenience is a worthy investment in avoiding injury and maximizing your performance later in the day.

A brief cool-down is also beneficial since it will loosen up tight muscle groups and enhance the recovery process. In particular, stretching and a few minutes of light aerobic activity help maintain increased blood flow and speed dispersion of lactic acid accumulated in the most fatigued muscles.

Focus on Technique Training over Strength Training

Many overuse injuries result from too much of a focus on strength training too early in an individual's climbing career. As advised throughout this book, it's fundamental to develop a high level of technical competence before jumping full bore into sport-specific training. Not only does good technique help reduce stress on the fingers and shoulders, but it also helps maximize economy of movement, and thus increases apparent strength on the rock.

Remember that two to four days per week of climbing will naturally produce rapid gains in sport-specific strength in beginners. Since tendons strengthen at a slower rate than muscles, novice climbers are not exempt from injury risk. With little experience, these new climbers have not yet developed the keen sense needed to distinguish good pain from bad pain. The number of climbers who become injured during their first year or two in the sport—as they quickly progress from, say, 5.5 to 5.10 (or higher)—is alarming. Awareness, maturity, and a prudent approach to training are therefore vital traits that must be fostered by all enthusiastic climbers.

Use Tape to Help Support Finger Tendons in the Most Stressful Situations and After Injury

Supportive taping of the finger tendon pulleys—it's most important to tape the base of the middle and ring fingers—helps lower the force load placed on the pulleys and may help prevent injury. Such taping, however, is not something you should use every day and on every climb. Subjecting the finger tendons and annular pulleys to gradually increasing levels of stress is what will make them stronger and able to function under higher and higher loads in the future. Taping all the time could thus have a negative impact on the long-term strength of this system.

Reserve use of prophylactic taping techniques (see page 141) for workouts or climbs that you expect will push the envelope of what the tendons have previously experienced. For instance, taping would be a wise measure for attempting a hardest-ever route, any climb known to possess injurious hold types (one-finger pockets, extreme crimps, and the like), or high-intensity training techniques such as campus or HIT training. Of course, individuals recovering from recent finger injuries should tape their fingers during the early stages of returning to climbing.

Proceed Cautiously through Dangerous Moves

An important sense to develop is that of knowing and managing movement through inherently dangerous moves or sequences. In recognizing that you are entering a dangerous sequence (say, a one-finger lock with poor feet) and in sensing that you are near injury on a move, you are empowered to either disengage from the move or cautiously manage through the sequence as expeditiously as possible. Clearly, it takes experience in such situations to develop this sense, but you can foster this important skill by knowing your body and the sensations you feel on various types of movements.

As a final note, a climber will often escape injury on the first attempt or pass through some heinous move, then get injured by attempting or rehearsing the painful move repeatedly. This is obviously a very unintelligent approach—no single route is worth getting injured and, possibly, laid up for months over. Bottom line: If you find yourself climbing into a move that feels overly painful or "injury scary," simply lower off and find a better route to enjoy.

Maintain Muscle Balance by Training Antagonist Muscle Groups

Training the antagonist muscles is one of the most overlooked—and most vital—parts of training for climbing. Muscle imbalances in the forearms, shoulders, and torso are primary factors in many overuse injuries. If you are serious about climbing your best and preventing injury, then you must commit to training the antagonist muscles twice per week.

The time and equipment involved are minimal. All the antagonist-muscle exercises described in chapter 3 can be performed at home with nothing more than a couple of dumbbells. As for the time commitment, it's less than twenty minutes, twice per week. I advise doing these exercises at the end of your weekday climbing or sport-specific workout. Keep the weights light to moderate, and do every single exercise outlined for the antagonist muscles of the upper body and forearms, as well as the handful of exercises for the core muscles of the torso (see page 73).

Don't Climb or Train More than Four Days Per Week

In most cases it is counterproductive to climb and train more than a total of four days per week. Consequently, if you are climbing four days a week on the rock, in the gym, or both combined, you should do no other sport-specific training during the three remaining days of the week. Even with three days' rest out of seven, your body will struggle to repair the microtraumas incurred to the tendons and muscles during your four climbing days. For this reason, it is wise to incorporate a training cycle such as the 4-3-2-1 Cycle (see page 63), since it provides a complete week off every few months. This is valuable catch-up time for your biological climbing machine! Finally, consider that in a pure strength- and power-training program (such as in a focused off-season training program), you may only be able to train two or three days per week, while you rest four or five.

Make Getting Proper Rest and Nutrition a Top Priority

Getting proper rest and nutrition seems like an obvious rule for a serious athlete, but I'm often surprised by the bad dietary and sleep habits possessed by some very serious climbers. Certainly, an occasional late night out or free day of eating and drinking whatever you like won't hurt (in fact, it's a great reward after a hard tick!). Consistent lack of sleep and poor nutrition, however, slows recovery between workouts and days of climbing, and undoubtedly makes you more vulnerable to injury.

Most important is good nutrition and a solid eight to nine hours of sleep in the day or two following an especially hard workout or day(s) of climbing. Consuming extra protein, a daily multivitamin, and antioxidant supplements will aid recovery and may help prevent the dreaded downward spiral into overtraining and injury.

Spreading Your Mental Wings for Peak Performance

Q: *I know you stress the importance of mental training for all climbers, yet my problems (and failures) on the rock almost always seem to revolve around weak, pumped-out muscles. What mental training can I do to make me feel stronger and climb more successfully?*

Your situation is common among the mass of climbers—that is, that pumped-out forearms seem to be the primary limiting factor. And you will only be able to

Pushing your limits (in anything) is a very mental thing—thus realizing your potential on the rock will only happen with well-developed mental prowess. Paula King on Predator (5.13c), Orange Crush Area, Rumney, New Hampshire. PHOTO: MICHAEL LANDKROON surpass the abilities of the mass of climbers when you come to recognize and act on the many factors that contribute to this muscular fatigue. These include but are not limited to: poor economy of movement, anxiety and overgripping, missed holds and rests due to inflexible thinking, and a tendency toward fearful thinking. All these mental issues produce premature fatigue and likely drain your energy reserves by 50 percent or more. Learning to think and act more effectively could very well double your apparent strength on the rock!

Let's examine four areas where mental training could help you unlock a higher level of performance. Consult chapter 4 for an entire toolbox of mental-training strategies.

Strive for Flexibility of Perspective

The first key strategy is flexibility of perspective. To break through a sticking point on a climb, you must get outside your current mind-set. Detach yourself from the situation and visualize it from a perspective outside yourself. View yourself attempting the climb from a dissociated on-TV perspective, and see yourself climbing bottom to top as well as downclimbing from the top to the ground. It's also a good idea to visualize how some great climber you know would attack the route—what tricks and tactics would he or she employ to send the route? Maybe dynoing past a long reach, searching out a hidden hold, or inventing a clever rest position? Make a game out of trying to transcend the block. Be creative and have fun, and all of a sudden the moves will begin to reveal themselves to you. You might not send the route that day, but you'll be making progress toward your goal.

Become a Reverse Paranoid

The second shift in thinking is to become what I call reverse paranoid. No matter what problems you encounter, believe that the route wants you to succeed (even if you are currently flailing miserably). In this way, view each failed attempt as a signpost directing you toward a better course of action instead of becoming obsessed with a single way the route must be done. Many climbers fail on routes they are physically capable of doing because they ignore the feedback that the route is giving them. Don't fall into this trap—embrace the feedback of your setbacks as clues toward your inevitable success.

Leverage a Mental Scrapbook of Past Successes

This third strategy is extremely powerful, and it's fundamental to achieving high levels of success in *any* field. Create a mental scrapbook of past successes that you can review on demand to fortify your confidence and persevere in the face of apparent failure. Relive in your mind's eye the process of some of your greatest accomplishments, both climbing and nonclimbing. Make these mental movies vivid and get inside them as if they were happening again at the present moment. *Feel* the exhilaration and joy of the accomplishment, then take that emotion and apply it to the difficult situation with which you are presently faced. Forge ahead wearing the mental armor of your past successes, and a whole new level of performance will begin to be revealed.

Strive to Develop Hanging-On Power

The final strategy is what I call hanging-on power. It's an attribute that all great climbers and high achievers (in any field) possess, and it enables them to persist beyond ordinary limits. Sometimes winning or succeeding isn't a matter of having more absolute strength or skill than others; it might just come down to being able to hang on and persevere longer.

Hanging-on power is an ability you develop from progressively subjecting yourself to greater and greater challenges that require higher levels of stick-to-itiveness. Just as in strengthening the muscles of your body, you strengthen mental muscle by challenging it in an incremental, progressive way. Bottom line: While some climbers give up at the first sign of adversity on a route (or after just a single day of failed attempts), the best climbers keep coming back and hanging on—mentally and physically—until they succeed. Foster this mental skill and you'll outperform the masses in anything you do!

And this leads us to one of the most powerful distinctions of this book—consider that these mental strategies are equally powerful for enhancing performance in your everyday life. Don't limit their use to climbing situations only; instead strive to view all aspects of your life through the flexible yet focused process-oriented perspective you've learned from climbing. The process of learning to climb 5.12 is a great metaphor for the process of climbing to a higher quality of life.

The classic HIT workout setup includes five evenly spaced HIT Strips and eight HIT Pinches. If you can't obtain the specialized HIT Strips, arrange sets of identical holds in a similar fashion.

Hypergravity Isolation Training (*HIT*)

Wall Setup

Use an overhanging bouldering wall of three-quarter-inch plywood at an angle of 45 to 55 degrees past vertical. HIT workouts on a 55-degree (past vertical) wall are significantly harder than those on the common 45-degree wall. If you are building a wall for HIT workouts, I advise a compromise angle of 50 degrees. Walls overhanging less than 45 degrees are not suggested for HIT workouts.

Sitting on the floor under the wall, mount the first HIT Strip at top-of-the-head height. Mount four more strips at 18- to 20-inch intervals. Two pinch holds are positioned above the first HIT Strip at shoulder width. The remaining pinch holds are mounted above the remaining HIT Strips at similar intervals.

Alternatively, you can rig a HIT-type setup using modular holds — if, that is, you have ten identical two-finger pocket holds, ten identical crimp holds, and ten identical pinch holds that are all usable on a 50-degree overhanging wall. Of course, if you don't have these holds, it will cost you as much or more than purchasing the complete HIT System from Nicros, Inc. Furthermore, use of the actual HIT Strips will help maintain your focus on the goal of using only the specific grip being trained, whereas using modular holds almost encourages you to break the sequence when you get pumped. You'll start grabbing holds other than the grip being trained and thus dilute the targeted nature of the HIT workout. Finally, the HIT Strips are optimized for a 50-degree wall and possess a safe, ergonomic radius of curvature to lower the pain factor when climbing with weight (important).

The Workout

Start with a thirty-minute warm-up comprised of gentle stretching and bouldering of increasing difficulty. The HIT workout trains seven basic grip positions: full crimp, half crimp, pinch, open hand, and the three teams of two-finger grips. Perform one or two sets for each grip position—those new to the HIT workout should begin with one set—beginning with the most difficult grip position for you. Most people work through the grips in this order: pinch, two-finger third team (pinkie and ring fingers), two-finger second team (index and middle fingers), two-finger first team (middle and ring fingers), full crimp, half crimp, and open hand. The entire HIT workout is done with open feet, meaning that you can place your feet on any holds on the wall. (See the sample HIT workouts below.)

Sample HIT Workouts—HIT Novice and HIT Advanced

grip to work	weight added* for HIT novice	weight added* for HIT advanced	reps** and rest interval
pinch	none	20 lbs.	<20 & 3 mins.
2-F 3rd team	none	20 lbs.	<20 & 3 mins.
2-F 2nd team	6 lbs.	40 lbs.	<20 & 3 mins.
2-F 1st team	8 lbs.	40 lbs.	<20 & 3 mins.
full crimp	10 lbs.	40 lbs.	<20 & 3 mins.
half crimp	10 lbs.	40 lbs.	<20 & 3 mins.
open hand	14 lbs.	40 lbs.	<20 & 3 mins.

*Lower weight or stop training at the first sign of tendon or joint pain.

**End every set at twenty reps or failure, whichever comes first. If you reach twenty reps, add weight for the next set and/or next workout. Keep a training log with the details of each HIT workout and use a stopwatch to keep rest intervals exact.

NOTE: Advanced climbers may want to perform two sets of training with each grip position. HIT Strips are available from Nicros (800–699–1975).

HIT Strips are optimized to train all the important grip positions—crimp, half crimp, open hand, and the three two-finger pocket teams. (The two-finger pocket "first team" is shown here.) Above the HIT Strip are two identical HIT pinch holds.

Sitting below the first HIT Strip, begin by gripping the right-hand pinch hold, then pull up and grab the next-higher left-hand pinch hold. Continue climbing with the next-higher right-hand pinch hold and the next-higher left-hand pinch hold until both hands are on the top two pinch holds. Begin descending immediately, alternating left and right pinch holds back down until you are holding the bottom two pinch holds—but keep going! Continue moving up and down the wall using alternating pinch holds until your grip fails. Upon stepping off the wall, use a stopwatch to time a rest of exactly three minutes before beginning the next set. Meanwhile, record the total number of reps or hand movements in your training notebook.

If you did more than twenty reps, you *must* add weight when training the pinch grip in the future. It's important to remember that doing more than twenty reps (ten movements per hand) will train anaerobic endurance, while training maximum grip strength requires adding weight to produce failure in ten or fewer

Here the author cranks an HIT set with the full crimp grip and 30 pounds around his waist.

PHOTO: ERIC MCCALLISTER

reps per hand. Add 5 pounds around your waist if you failed at between twenty and twenty-five total reps. Otherwise, add 10 pounds around your waist for the next set on the pinch grips. To add weight, buy a couple of 5- and 10-pound weight belts at your local sports store or, alternatively, use a large fanny pack and added 2-pound diver's weights (available at most scuba stores). Elite climbers may wish to purchase a 20- or 40-pound weight vest in addition to a couple of weight belts.

After your three-minute rest, proceed immediately with a second set of pinch grips. (HIT novices should proceed to the next grip position, forgoing a second set.) Climb up and down on the pinch holds in the same fashion as the first set. Upon failure, time another three-minute rest, then move on to the next grip position—probably the two-finger pocket third team.

Begin the next set by using the two-finger third team to grab the two pocket holds on the bottom HIT Strip. As with the pinch grip, climb the pocket holds up and down using exclusively this two-finger pocket team on alternating HIT Strips (or on identically sized and spaced two-finger pockets). Continue to failure, then rest for exactly three minutes before performing the second set with this grip. Record the total number of hand movements as well as the amount of weight added, if any.

After completing the second set of this two-finger team, move on to the next grip position. Continue executing the HIT workout through the remaining grip positions while taking just a three-minute rest between each set. It's vital that you limit the rest to exactly three minutes, and record the number of hand movements and the weight used (if any) for each grip and set. This information will guide your next HIT workout, and I guarantee the records will quantify definitive gains in your grip strength in the sessions that follow!

This completes your HIT workout, though you may wish to do a few sets of weighted pull-ups or some lock-off exercises to complete your strength training of the upper body. Do no further finger training, however. As a cool-down, do ten minutes of light bouldering. You will likely need two or four days of quality rest and sound nutrition in order to supercompensate to 110 percent!

HIT Principles and Tips

- Each set must be maximum intensity and produce failure in twenty hand movements or less. Add weight if you achieve more than twenty reps.

- No stopping or chalking during a set. Climb briskly and without hesitation. Consider using a spotter so you can keep moving confidently up to the point of failure.

- Try to climb through the reps with normal foot movements and body turns. Smaller footholds (approximately half an inch to 1 inch in depth) are better, but too much thought on footwork will slow you down. Most importantly, keep the footwork simple—the goal is to train the fingers, not footwork and technique.

- Rest breaks between sets must be exactly three minutes. Use a stopwatch and stick to the planned order and schedule of exercises. This way you can quantify and track your finger strength! If you're sloppy on the length of rests, the numbers become meaningless.

- Keep a training book in which you log each set, weight added, and reps performed. This way you'll always know what weight you need for a given set and you can easily track your gains (weight and rep increases) from workout to workout.

- Always do your HIT workout in the same order, and never perform more than two sets per grip position! There will be no added stimuli, and you'll only dig yourself a deeper hole to recover from—that is, you'll need more days to recovery—thus risking injury. HIT novices should only perform one set of each grip position.

- Tape your fingers using the X method. This is imperative as the weight added begins to exceed 20 pounds. It will also increase the skin comfort level, allowing you to push the envelope a bit further. Sand down the HIT Strips or holds if the texture causes pain that prevents you from completing each set to muscular failure.

- Increase rest days if you find your HIT reps and weights decreasing. If you ever feel weak on the rock after a HIT cycle, it's due to insufficient rest. Remember that it can take as much as four to seven days to recover from severe central fatigue.

- Cycle on and off of HIT every two weeks, or employ weighted HIT workouts only during the three-week maximal-strength phase of the 4-3-2-1 Cycle.

Anaerobic Endurance (A-E) Training Using a HIT Workout System

In addition to use in training maximum strength, the HIT workout system can be used in a different way to effectively train anaerobic endurance (i.e. endurance of grip strength). The A-E training protocol involves heightening the "training load" by increasing the number of reps (hand movements), not by adding weight.

In doing an A-E HIT workout, the goal is to climb up and down the HIT Strips using a single grip position for a total of thirty to fifty hand movements. The rest period between sets should be at least five minutes—not the three minutes used in the maximum strength HIT workout. Begin with the weakest grip (usually pinch) and perform one (HIT novice) or two sets of thirty to fifty reps for each of the seven grip positions discussed above. In A-E training the goal is not absolute muscular failure, but instead to take the muscles in and out of the anaerobic energy mode in an interval training fashion.

Again, it's vital that your track your A-E HIT workout on paper. Record in a notebook the number of reps (total hand movements) performed in each of the seven to fourteen sets. Upon completion of all the grip positions, perform any supplemental training of the larger pull muscles (pull-up and lock off exercises), then wrap up your workout with a good cool down of light bouldering and stretching.

Route Pyramids

Pyramid of Climbs to 5.10a
Fill in route name and date of redpoint.
One route per block.

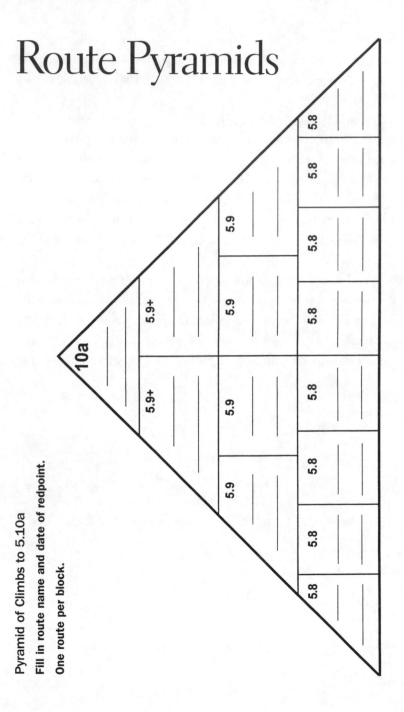

Pyramid of Climbs to 5.11a

Fill in route name and date of redpoint.

One route per block.

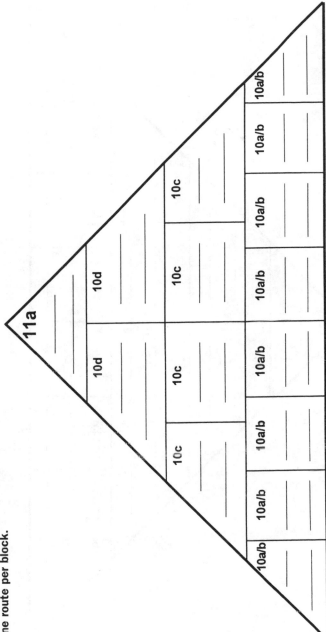

Pyramid of Climbs to 5.12a
Fill in route name and date of redpoint.
One route per block.

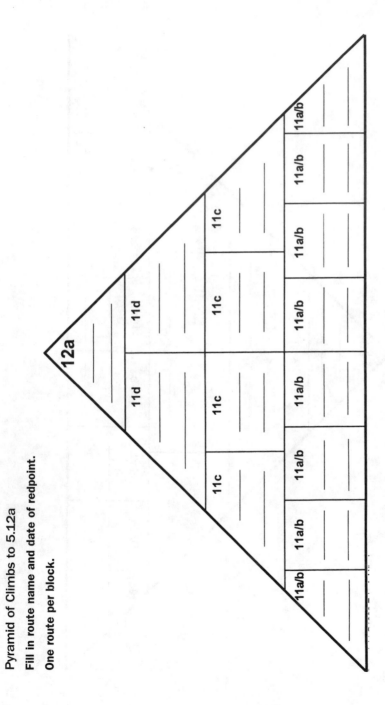

Pyramid of Climbs to 5.13a

Fill in route name and date of redpoint.

One route per block.

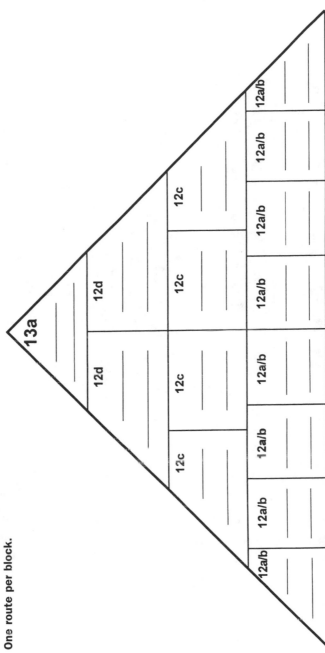

Glossary

The following is a compilation of some of the technical terms and jargon used throughout this book.

aerobic(s): any physical activity deriving energy from the breakdown of glycogen in the presence of oxygen, thus producing little or no lactic acid, enabling an athlete to continue exercise much longer

aggro: short for "aggressive"

anaerobic: energy production in the muscles involving the breakdown of glycogen in the absence of oxygen; a by-product called lactic acid is formed, resulting in rapid fatigue and cessation of physical activity

anaerobic endurance: the ability to continue moderate- to high-intensity activity over a period of time; climbers often use the scientifically incorrect terms *power endurance* or *power stamina* to describe anaerobic endurance

antagonist: a muscle providing an opposing force to the primary muscles of action

antioxidants: substances (for example, vitamins and minerals) proven to oppose oxidation and inhibit or neutralize free radicals

arousal: an internal state of alertness or excitement

backstepping: outside edging on a foothold that is behind you while climbing a move with your side to the wall

beta: any prior information about a route, including sequence, rests, gear, clips, and so forth

biological value (BV): a method for evaluating protein sources; a high-BV protein source has a high percentage of nutrients actually absorbed from the human intestine as opposed to excreted

blocked practice: a practice routine in which a specific task is practiced repeatedly, such as while working a crux move or sequence

bouldering: variable practice of climbing skills performed without a belay rope at the base of a cliff or on small boulders

campus (or campusing): climbing an overhanging section of rock or artificial wall with no feet, usually in a dynamic left-hand, right-hand, left-hand sequence

catabolic: a breaking-down process in the body, such as a muscle breakdown during intense exercise or the like

chronic: a long-term disorder; not acute

contact strength: the rate at which peak strength can be summoned in gripping a handhold

crimp grip: the most natural (and stressful) way to grip a rock hold, characterized by hyperextension of the first joint in the fingers and nearly full contraction of the second joint

crux: the hardest move, or sequence of moves, on a route

deadpoint: the "high" position of a dynamic move where, for a moment, all motion stops

detox: to shake out, rest, and recover from a pump

drop-knee: an exaggerated backstep in which one knee is dropped toward the ground whereas the other is pointing up, resulting in a stable chimneylike position, especially on overhanging rock

dynamic move: an explosive leap for a hold otherwise out of reach

dyno: short for "dynamic"

eccentric muscle movement: a muscle action in which the muscle resists as it is forced to lengthen

epicondylitis: inflammation of the tendon origins of the forearm extensors (lateral) or flexors (medial) near the elbow

ergogenic: performance enhancing

flagging: a climbing technique in which one foot is crossed behind the other to avoid barn-dooring and to improve balance

flash: to climb a route on the first try without ever having touched it, but with the aid of beta

flash pump: a rapid, often vicious, muscular pump resulting from strenuous training or climbing without first performing a proper (gradual) warm-up

G-Tox: a technique that uses gravity to help speed recovery from a forearm pump; it involves alternating (every five to ten seconds) the position of the resting arm between the normal hanging-at-your-side position and a raised-hand position above your shoulder

glycemic index: a scale that classifies how the ingestion of various foods affects blood sugar levels in comparison to the ingestion of straight glucose

glycogen: compound chains of glucose stored in the muscle and liver for use during aerobic or anaerobic exercise

gripped: extremely scared

hangdogging: "climbing" a route, usually bolt to bolt, with the aid of the rope to hang and rest

heel hook: the use of the heel on a hold, usually near chest level, to aid in pulling and balance

honed: in extremely good shape; with low body fat

Hypergravity Isolation Training (HIT): a highly refined and specific method of training maximal finger strength and upper-body power via climbing on identical finger holds (isolation) with greater than body weight (hypergravity); also known as Hörst Isolation Training

hypertrophy: enlargement in size (for example, muscular hypertrophy)

insulin: a hormone that decreases blood glucose level by driving glucose from the blood into muscle and fat cells

isometric: a muscular contraction resulting in no shortening of the muscle (no movement)

killer: extraordinarily good

kinesthetic: the sense derived from muscular contractions and limb movements

lactic acid: an acid by-product of the anaerobic metabolism of glucose during intense muscular exercise

lunge: an out-of-control dynamic move; a jump for a far-off hold

macronutrients: basic nutrients needed for energy, cell growth, and organ function (such as carbohydrates, fat, and protein)

manky: of poor quality, as in *manky finger jam* or *manky protection placement*

maximal strength: the peak force of a muscular contraction, irrespective of the time element

mental practice: practice in which you visualize successful execution without overt physical practice

modeling: a learning technique in which you watch, then attempt, a skill as performed properly by another person

motor learning: set of internal processes associated with practice or experience, leading to a relatively permanent gain in performance capability

motor skill: a skill whose primary determinant of success is the movement component itself

motor unit: a motor neuron, together with a group of muscle cells stimulated in an all-or-nothing response

muscular endurance: the length of time a given level of power can be maintained

on-sight: when a route is climbed on the first try and with absolutely no prior information of any kind

open-hand grip: a safer grip involving only slight flexion of the first two joints of the fingers

power: a measure of both force and speed (speed equals distance multiplied by time) of a muscular contraction through a given range of motion (note that technically the term *finger power* is meaningless, since the fingers normally don't move when gripping the rock)

psyched: raring to go or very happy

pumped: when the muscles become engorged with blood due to extended physical exertion

random practice: a practice sequence in which tasks from several classes are experienced in random order over consecutive trials

recommended dietary allowances (RDA): the daily quantities of specific vitamins, minerals, and protein that have been judged adequate for maintenance of good nutrition in the U.S. population, developed by the Food and Nutrition Board of the National Academy of Sciences

redpoint: lead climbing a route from bottom to top in one push

reminiscence effect: the phenomenon of enhanced motor skill and performance after an extended time-off period from climbing and training

schema: a set of rules, usually developed and applied unconsciously by the motor system in the brain and spinal cord, relating how to move and adjust muscle forces, body positions, and so forth, given the parameters at hand, such as steepness of the rock, friction qualities, holds being used, and type of terrain

send it: an emphatic statement to someone encouraging him or her to hang in and finish a route without falling

sharp end: the lead climber's end of the rope

shred: to do really well, or to dominate

skill: the ability to bring about an end result with maximal certainty, minimal energy, and minimal time

sport climbing: usually refers to any indoor or outdoor climbing on bolt-protected routes

spotter: a person designated to slow the fall of a boulderer, with the main goal of keeping the boulderer's head from hitting the ground

tendinitis: a disorder involving the inflammation of a tendon and synovial membrane at a joint

tendon: a white fibrous cord of dense, regular connective tissue that attaches muscle to bone

trad: short for "traditional climber"—someone who prefers routes with natural protection instead of bolts

training effect: a basic principle of exercise science that states that adaptation occurs from an exercise only in those parts or systems of the body stressed by the exercise

transfer of learning: the gain or loss in proficiency on one task as a result of practice or experience on another task

tweak: to injure, as in *tweaked finger tendon*

variable practice: practice in which many variations of a class of actions are performed; the opposite of blocked practice

visualization: controlled and directed imagery that can be used for awareness building, monitoring and self-regulation, healing, and, most importantly, mental programming for good performances

wired: known well, as in *wired route*

working: practicing the moves on a difficult route via toprope or hangdogging

Further Reading

Brand-Miller, Jennie, et al. *The Glucose Revolution: The Authoritative Guide to the Glycemic Index*. New York: Marlowe & Company, 1999.

Burke, Edmund R. *Optimal Muscle Recovery*. Garden City Park, N.Y.: Avery Publishing Group, 1999.

Colgan, Michael. *Optimum Sports Nutrition*. Ronkonkoma, N.Y.: Advanced Research Press, 1993.

Garfield, Charles A. *Peak Performance*. New York: Warner Books, 1985.

Goddard, Dale, and Udo Neumann. *Performance Rock Climbing*. Mechanicsburg, Pa.: Stackpole Books, 1993.

Hörst, Eric J. *Training for Climbing*. Guilford, Conn.: Globe Pequot Press, 2003.

—— *Mental Wings: A Seven-Step Life-Elevating Program for Uncommon Success*. www.MentalWings.com, 2003.

Long, John. *Advanced Rock Climbing*. Guilford, Conn.: Globe Pequot Press, 1997.

Meagher, Jack. *Sports Massage*. New York: Station Hill, 1990.

Orlick, Terry. *In Pursuit of Excellence*. Champaign, Ill.: Human Kinetics, 1990.

Sagar, Heather Reynolds. *Climbing Your Best*. Mechanicsburg, Pa.: Stackpole Books, 2001.

Schmidt, Richard B. *Motor Learning and Performance: From Principles to Practice*. Champaign, Ill.: Human Kinetics, 1991.

Fitness Evaluation

This ten-part evaluation is strenuous. Perform a complete warm-up before proceeding, and rest extensively between tests. Take this test annually to gauge your changes in conditioning for climbing. Please send me a copy of your initial test results so they can be included in an ongoing statistical study.

Test 1: One set maximum number of pull-ups. Do this test on a standard pull-up bar with your palms away and hands shoulder width apart. Do not bounce, and be sure to go up and down the whole way.
Evaluation: Total number of pull-ups in a single set to failure.
*Results:*_____

Test 2: One repetition maximum pull-up. Do a single pull-up with a 10-pound weight clipped to your harness. Rest for three minutes, then add 10 more pounds and repeat. (If you are very strong, begin with a 20-pound weight and increase at 10- to 20-pound increments.) Continue in this fashion until you have added more weight than you can pull up.
Evaluation: The maximum amount of added weight successfully lifted for a single pull-up divided by your body weight.
*Results:*_____

Test 3: One-arm lock-off. Start with a standard chin-up (palms facing), then lock off at the top on one arm and let go with the other.
Evaluation: Length of time in the lock-off before your chin drops below the bar.
Results: Right arm_____ Left arm _____

Test 4: One set maximum number of Frenchies. Perform the exercise as described on page 56. Remember, each cycle consists of three pull-ups separated by the three different lock-off positions, which are held for five seconds. Have a partner time your lock offs.
Evaluation: The number of cycles (or part of) completed in a single set.
Results: _____

Test 5: One set maximum number of fingertip pull-ups on a three-quarter-inch (19-millimeter) edge. Perform this exercise as in Test 1 except on a fingerboard edge or doorjamb of approximately the stated size.

Evaluation: The number of fingertip pull-ups done in a single go.

*Results:*_____

Test 6: Lock off in the top position of a fingertip pull-up (three-quarter-inch or 19-millimeter edge) for as long as possible.

Evaluation: Length of time in the lock-off until your chin drops below the edge.

Results: _____

Test 7: Straight-armed hang from a standard pull-up bar. Place your hands shoulder width apart with palms facing away.

Evaluation: Length of time you can hang on the bar before muscle failure.

*Results:*_____

Test 8: One set maximum number of sit-ups. Perform these on a pad or carpeted floor with your knees bent at approximately 90 degrees and your feet flat on the floor with nothing anchoring them. Cross your arms over your chest and perform each sit-up until your elbows touch your knees or thighs.

Evaluation: Number of sit-ups you can perform without stopping. Do them in a controlled manner (no bouncing off the floor).

*Results:*_____

Test 9: Wall split as described on page 49. Be sure that your rear end is no more than 6 inches from the wall.

Evaluation: Position your legs so they are equidistant from the floor and measure the distance from your heels to the floor.

Results: _____

Test 10: High-step stretch as shown on page 50. Stand facing a wall with one foot flat on the floor with toes touching the wall. Lift the other leg up to the side as high as possible without any aid from the hands.

Evaluation: Measure the height of your step off the floor and divide it by your height.

*Results:*_____

Questionnaire

1. Name _____
   Address _____
   City/state/zip _____
   Country _____
   e-mail _____

2. Age _____ Sex _____

3. Height _____ Weight _____ Percent body fat (if known) _____

4. Previous sports background _____

5. Number of years climbing _____

6. Preferred type of climbing (sport, trad, bouldering, big wall) _____

7. Current on-sight lead ability (75 percent success rate at what level) _____

8. Hardest redpoint (worked route) _____

9. Are you currently doing sport-specific training for climbing? _____
   If so, which exercises do you use (circle): fingerboard, campus training, HIT, system wall, other _____

10. Do you have a home climbing wall? _____

11. How often do you climb indoors (days per month)? _____

12. Do you belong to a climbing gym? _____
    If so, which one? _____

13. Have you ever participated in a climbing competition? _____

14. Have you ever been injured while climbing or training for climbing?
_____
If so, describe? _____

15. Approximately how many days per year do you climb? _____

16. How many different climbing areas have you visited in the past twelve
months? _____

17. What are your goals in this sport? _____

18. What chapter or part of *How to Climb* 5.12 do you like best?
_____

19. What subjects would you like expanded upon in my next book?
_____

20. What climber would you like to see interviewed with regard to his or her
training and climbing?
_____

Send your Fitness Evaluation and Questionnaire to the address below. Include a self-addressed stamped envelope and I'll send you some free climbing stickers. Thank you!

Contact information:

Eric J. Hörst
P.O. Box 8633
Lancaster, PA 17604
www.TrainingForClimbing.com

Index

friction, 8
froggies, 49

G

glycemic index (GI), 136–38
goals, 80–81
grip positions, 121
G-tox, 123–25

H

hand pronators, 60
hanging knee lifts, 58
herbal supplements, 134–36
high steps, 50
Hypergravity Isolation Training
  (HIT), 69

I

indoor climbing, 28, 41–42, 130, 132
injuries, 72, 140–42, 147–50

L

lat pulldown, 55
lat stretches, 51

M

mental preparation, 37
  ANSWER Sequence, 98–99
  confidence, 82, 84
  control and poise, 96
  discipline, 82
  fears, 87–88, 90–91
  focus, 94–95
  goals, 80–81
  motivation, 79–80
  peak performance and, 150,
    152–53

preclimb rituals, 87
pressure, 91–92
relaxation, 92–93
self-talk, 100–101
visualization, 84–86
modeling, 34
motivation, 79–80
motor performance maps, 25–27
muscle balance, 72–74, 149–50

N

nutrition, 12, 75, 134–38, 150

O

on-sighting, 36–37, 106, 108–13

P

performance, 6–13
  evaluating, 14, 16–21
  skill development, 23–28, 32–34,
    36–37, 39–43
performance days, 25
poise, 96
practice days, 25
preclimb rituals, 87
preparation, 5–6
pressure, 91–92
Progressive Relaxation Sequence,
  92–93
pull-ups, 54
push-muscle exercises, 72–74
push-ups, 73

R

random skill practice, 41–42
recovery, 72, 74–77, 129–30
redpoints, 113–17

About the Author

A n accomplished climber for more than twenty-five years, Eric J. Hörst (pronounced *Hirst*) has ascended cliffs all across the United States and Europe. He has established more than 400 first ascents, primarily on his home cliffs in the eastern U.S.

A student and teacher of climbing performance, Eric has helped train hundreds of climbers, and his training books and concepts have spread to climbers in more than forty-five countries. He is widely recognized for his innovative practice methods and training tools, and he has been a training products design consultant for Nicros, Inc., since 1994.

Eric is also the author of *Flash Training* (Falcon, 1994) and *Training for Climbing* (Falcon, 2003). He has written more than two dozen magazine articles on the subject, appeared on numerous TV broadcasts, and his techniques have been featured in such magazines as *Climbing, Rock & Ice, Outside, Men's Health, Muscle Media,* and *Men's Journal.*

Eric J. Hörst on the first ascent of Logotherapy (5.13b), Bubba City, New River Gorge, West Virginia.

PHOTO: ERIC MCCALLISTER

Eric lives in Lancaster, Pennsylvania, with his wife, Lisa Ann, and his sons, Cameron and Jonathan.

ACCESS: It's every climber's concern

The Access Fund, a national, non-profit climbers organization, works to keep climbing areas open and to conserve the climbing environment. Need help with closures? land acquisition? legal or land management issues? funding for trails and other projects? starting a local climbers' group? CALL US! Climbers can help preserve access by being committed to Leave No Trace (minimum-impact) practices. Here are some simple guidelines:

- **ASPIRE TO "LEAVE NO TRACE"** especially in environmentally sensitive areas like caves. Chalk can be a significant impact on dark and porous rock—don't use it around historic rock art. Pick up litter, and leave trees and plants intact.

- **DISPOSE OF HUMAN WASTE PROPERLY** Use toilets whenever possible. If toilets are not available, dig a "cat hole" at least six inches deep and 200 feet from any water, trails, campsites, or the base of climbs. *Always pack out toilet paper.* On big wall routes, use a "poop tube" and carry waste up and off with you (the old "bag toss" is now illegal in many areas).

- **USE EXISTING TRAILS** Cutting switchbacks causes erosion. When walking off-trail, tread lightly, especially in the desert where cryptogamic soils (usually a dark crust) take thousands of years to form and are easily damaged. Be aware that "rim ecologies" (the clifftop) are often highly sensitive to disturbance.

- **BE DISCRETE WITH FIXED ANCHORS** *Bolts are controversial and are not a convenience*—don't place 'em unless they are *really* necessary. Camouflage all anchors. Remove unsightly slings from rappel stations (better to use steel chain or welded cold shuts). Bolts sometimes can be used proactively to protect fragile resources—consult with your local land manager.

- **RESPECT THE RULES** and speak up when other climbers don't. Expect restrictions in designated wilderness areas, rock art sites, caves, and to protect wildlife, especially nesting birds of prey. *Power drills are illegal in wilderness and all national parks.*

- **PARK AND CAMP IN DESIGNATED AREAS** Some climbing areas require a permit for overnight camping.

- **MAINTAIN A LOW PROFILE** Leave the boom box and day-glo clothing at home—the less climbers are heard and seen, the better.

- **RESPECT PRIVATE PROPERTY** Be courteous to land owners. Don't climb where you're not wanted.

- **JOIN THE ACCESS FUND** To become a member, make a tax-deductible donation of $35.

The Access Fund

Preserving America's Diverse Climbing Resources
P.O. Box 17010
Boulder, CO 80308
303.545.6772 • www.accessfund.org